# WHY NOT ASK?

## A CONVERSATION ABOUT GETTING MORE

### CHRISTINE MCKAY

MAVERICK
PRODUCTIONS INC

*To all the people who believed in me,*
*when I didn't believe in myself.*

# CONTENTS

## PART III

# FOREWORD

When I first learned that I would be interviewing an expert negotiator for a podcast, I will admit, I was a bit skeptical. After all, I'm an authority in the health and wellness space, and negotiations feels so, well... stuffy. But my publicist insisted that I give this woman a shot, and my publicist has never steered me wrong. So, I put the podcast interview in my schedule and logged-in when it was time.

Christine McKay was not at all what I expected. Far from the stuffed shirt, stiff negotiation expert I'd imagined, she was a fun, energetic force, and the conversation with her was one I truly enjoyed.

From her down-to-earth style to her purple hair, to her engaging sense of humor, Christine made me think about negotiation in a whole new light. Our conversation helped me recognize that we are all in constant negotiation without realizing it.

Co-parenting is a negotiation.

Working with clients is a negotiation.

Signing a contract for a TV show is a negotiation.

Heck, even being interviewed for a podcast is a negotiation.

Christine helped me see that I had been putting negotiation in a "that's someone else's job" box, and inspired me to take a good, hard look at how often I was disempowering myself with that belief. That interview was a lightbulb moment that motivated me to improve and refine my own negotiation skills for all aspects of my life – both business and personal.

*Why Not Ask* is the quintessential handbook on real-world negotiations. Whether you're negotiating your position at a new job, figuring out the best way to get your kid to bed on time, or talking to a dealer about buying a new car, Christine helps you to understand that, in truth, negotiation is a conversation about a relationship, and provides the tools to empower you to get the best deal done.

With her unique and insightful understanding that negotiation is all about relationship building – both in the business world and in life – Christine's approach is what we all need more of. Our interview, and this book, had me renegotiate my views on negotiation. It will do the same for you.

Jillian Michaels, Miami 2021

# NEGOTIATION STYLES PREVIEW

What is negotiation?

Negotiation is something we learn as children, and we are masterful at it when we are seven. Over time, we learn that a certain style works better for us than others. That style becomes our default style and one which we rely on most as adults. There are times, though, when we move out of our default style because we are triggered to the *fight-or-flight* reflex, or to the *tend-and-befriend* instinct.

This is a topic that deserves a whole book to itself, which is why I am covering it in the upcoming book ***How You Ask Matters: Turning Negotiation Styles into Strategies.***

If you want to find out more about your negotiation style, visit my website at www.VennNegotiation.com and take the Negotiation Styles Quiz to find out which one you are.

Here, I'm just giving you a sneak peek so you can identify the different styles we all use.

Research from a university study found that there are four negotiation styles. The four styles are:

*Champion, Maverick, Benefactor,* and *Ambassador.*

We've used all four of these styles at different times of our lives, and many of us have tried to fit into one of these styles. We all default to one of these styles more readily than any of the others. We tend to use them without thinking about them. But we can also shift into other styles depending on the situation. Figuring out how to use these different styles in a way that creates more goodwill and reasons to do business together was one of the biggest challenges I've had in my years as a negotiator.

The 'Champion' is the reason why some people absolutely abhor and are terrified of negotiating 'The Champion' is a champion for themselves. They see negotiation as a battlefield or as a battle. They go into that battle fully armed and fully armored. It is all about annihilating their opponent. They will often agree to accept terms in a deal that are not in their best interest if they think it will conquer their opponent. Theirs is a very emotional and aggressive style. 'Champions' have a bullying style; the style that is this is the way it's going to be, I don't care. They can throw things. They can scream and yell; they can be very demeaning in their language.

When somebody adopts this 'Champion' style, they often don't have leverage or power. They think that screaming and yelling and calling you names is going to get them somewhere. That's why they don't have the leverage. They don't believe in what they're asking for, and that triggers them.

The 'Maverick' is what I sometimes call a checklist negotiator. They are similar to the champion in that they negotiate one issue at a time. One of the most significant differences between the 'Maverick' and the 'Champion' is that they are not looking to conquer their counterpart. They don't care about what is going on with their counterpart. They're very focused on getting what they want out of the negotiation. About 55% of negotiators are 'Mavericks.' It is a very common style. The 'Maverick' may have a checklist, they've gone through, and they've done an exercise.

'Mavericks' may see themselves as having failed in the negotiation for not getting everything on their list. They would see themselves as failing if they got less than 50% of what was on their agenda. It depends on what they're negotiating and negotiating for regarding how they'll think about their list.

The 'Benefactor' is an interesting style because it's focused on what appears to be relationship preservation. The 'Benefactor' will often agree to things in a negotiation that may or may not be in their best interests because they think they have to preserve the relationship. Now, the challenge with this style, is that the 'Benefactor' is focused on relationships and is very conflict avoidant. Because they're very conflict-avoidant, they will agree to almost anything to get the negotiation over with because they see negotiation as conflict.

The 'Ambassador' is probably the most gifted in the negotiation process. The 'Ambassador' is more focused on the original meaning of win-win. I describe a win-win, at least in the original intent, as an egg.

If you have an egg and three people who want the egg, what do you do?

Well, if it's just a raw egg, if you break it, it's all going to heck in a hand-basket. You can't do anything with it. It's just goo and gross. You can use it for trash and compost, maybe. But that's it, you've diminished this point, this thing, into something that is not usable by very many.

You could boil the egg and divide it into three. 'Champions,' 'Mavericks,' and 'Benefactors,' will look at the egg and think, "I have to split the egg evenly amongst three people. I will boil the egg and divide it into thirds."

The 'Ambassador' will naturally look at the egg and say,

"Oh, no, no, I can take a pin, and I can poke a hole in the egg, drain the yolk and the egg white out, then I have the shell. Then I can separate the whites from the yolk. I can give the yolk to somebody who's needing to glaze a cake. I can provide the white to somebody who's selling beaten egg whites. I can sell the shell to somebody who's doing art or who wants to compost."

This is how the 'Ambassador' creates a win-win from something that looks like it was one thing. The 'Ambassador' equally divided it in three ways, to three people, who had three different objectives for using the egg. The 'Ambassador' is very much about finding ways to create an egg out of that situation.

How do you create a solution and separate something into multiple parts that add value to all of the parties at the table? One of the challenges for 'Ambassadors' is that they love to think about things and make issues out of non-issues because they like that complexity level. About 25 to 30% of negotiators are 'Ambassadors.'

Now you understand more about the communication attributes of the four key negotiation styles: 'Maverick,' 'Champion,' 'Benefactor,' and 'Ambassador.'

Which one are you?

# INTRODUCTION

## MY NEGOTIATION STORY

*Negotiation is a conversation about a relationship, and you can't win a relationship.*
*But, you can get more value out of it.*

My experience at Harvard was an unusual one. I was the only woman in my class to have three kids. When I graduated, my daughters were still young. My oldest daughter completed sixth grade the year that I graduated. My ex-husband was suing me for custody while I was there. I didn't get to enjoy my time at Harvard the way that I would have liked. After school, my kids were home without me. I was always worried that somebody would come and take them for me. I would finish class, then I'd run home as fast as I possibly could.

One of the things about Harvard is the community that is built by being with like-minded students. Because of my hectic schedule, balancing being a parent and being a student, I missed the ability to connect with more of my classmates. There was nobody like me at Harvard, so it was very challenging at times. But, nonetheless, it was an amazing education. I had the opportunity to learn, especially negotiation, which was one of my favorite classes of all time. I had the chance to learn from the professors who were involved in the writing of *Getting to Yes*, and the Harvard Program on negotiation. It was one of the vanguard programs that put the topic of negotiation on the global map in terms of being a subject area to study and research.

Through the case study process, studying the stories of people who had effectively negotiated agreements, and those who hadn't. I learned a tremendous amount. One of the great things that Harvard taught was the process around negotiation, and the importance of preparation in the negotiation effort.

Little did I know how much I would need that preparation, and what the program contributed to my personal life.

Even today, over twenty years after my Harvard experience, the skills I learned in negotiation still hold true.

As a single mother, as an ex-wife, as a businesswoman, and in my current marriage; I use those negotiation skills in every aspect of my life.

I know that the simplicity of negotiating an agreement is not always easy. I also know that, armed with the tools in this book, negotiating a solution that empowers everyone is possible.

If you're nervous about negotiation, or you absolutely hate it, are afraid of it - I'm going to provide tools and techniques in this book to help you get through the negotiation process. If it works well, you might even get to enjoy it a little bit more.

After all, you can't get what you want unless you ask for it. So, why not ask?

## How to Think About Negotiation

Many people think that negotiation is something you're born to do and that it's this personality thing. I don't believe that. I believe that we are all excellent negotiators.

We all used to be excellent negotiators. Often, when I'm doing a program, I ask the audience the question: who in here has a parent?

Of course, everyone raises their hand.

The reality is that if you were a child, and you were, and you still might be, you are an excellent negotiator. The problem is that over time, we start hearing the word *'no'*. And we have different experiences that accumulate in us and on us. Experiences that weigh on us causing us to change our behavior and become fearful in some cases of asking for more of what we want. Because we assume that we're going to hear the word *'no'*.

Some people have physical situations that reinforce that, whether through emotional abuse or physical abuse, the fear of conflict and negotiation is often seen as combative, intimidating, and therefore threatening. We have lots of bullies in the world, and we, for some reason, continue to reward bullies as they are negotiating. My view is that if somebody is a bully to you while you're negotiating, get up and walk out of the room because they're going to be an even bigger bully to you after you sign a deal with them. Don't do business with bullies. It's pretty simple.

For me, I believe that negotiation is something that we're all inherently capable of doing, and we're all gifted at it. If you look at it over time, from the time you were a child to where you are today, and you look at all the things you negotiated over the course of your life, you'll find you've had more people that have answered *'yes'* than you have had people answer *'no'*. You just choose to focus on the times you heard *No* and not the *Yeses*. There's no need to be afraid to ask for what you want because you're likely going to get it.

## How I Learned About Negotiation

I feel like I'm offering something different from what you hear from many people who talk about negotiation. Most people who talk about the topic of negotiation fall into some specific camps. So you have academics, most of whom are law school professors or business school professors. You have people who were on SWAT teams or are hostage negotiators; you have international trade negotiators, and you have people in sales. And there's a significant population of people who think that negotiation is just sales. But it's not. It's so much more than that. Most people who teach negotiation teach it at a corporate level. They talk in terms of gimmicks and things that are tricks and how to game the negotiation. For me, negotiation is about relationships.

I essentially started my adult life as a 19-year-old pregnant unwed teen living in the back of my 1972 Chrysler Newport with my black cat Athena. Shortly after I quit living in the back of my car, when I was pregnant, I met a woman named Roxanne Uken. She challenged me to draw a picture and put four goals on a piece of paper. I did; only one of them, I remember. That goal was to go to Harvard.

She asked me, "What do you want to do?" Then, she offered to help me.

This was pivotal.

I accepted help when people brought food to my house.

I accepted help when people offered to guide me.

I accepted the help.

Part of *accepting* help is not *expecting* help, but being open to assistance when offered to you.

The first day that I went to the welfare office, somebody asked me what I was going to do. I blurted out - I was going to go to Harvard. They started laughing at me. I was a statistic. I was a loser. I'd never get out of the system they told me. I walked in feeling confident. I walked out knowing I was the failure they'd described me as. The things that I had to do, the steps I had to negotiate, the people I had to negotiate with, and the things I had to negotiate for on behalf of myself and my children were significant. I realized that nobody had taught me how to do that, I was flying by the seat of my pants, and it frustrated me.

I went from homeless to Harvard, very slowly. It was an 11-year process to get there. After moving out of my car, I met a guy that I ended up getting married to, and I ended up having two more kids. I had three daughters by the age of 22. We were incredibly poor, often buying groceries at the food bank. We would sometimes have to boil water on our stove for our kids' baths because we couldn't afford to heat in the house. I decided I wanted a different life. The day my oldest wanted lunch, and all I had in my house was a single can of tomato soup, and she cried because tomato soup hurt her mouth. I picked her up, and I practically shoved her into the cupboard to show her that was all I had to feed her. I said to myself; I cannot keep doing this.

At the time, my husband didn't believe that women should be educated and did not support me getting an education. He was pretty aggressive about that approach, and him having the right to tell me what to do and what not to do. When I decided to apply to and go to community college, Berkshire Community College, it was a risk for me to do that. I was only allowed to study when my daughters were sleeping, and he was either sleeping or wasn't home. I earned a 4.0 GPA and was awarded a full scholarship to Rensselaer Polytechnic Institute. When I got to campus one day for class registration and orientation, I said to myself, "this will be a lot easier on my own than it is with him."

I went home, I told him that I was taking the girls and we were leaving. And that's what I did.

Rensselaer was phenomenal in helping me to arrange on-campus housing and doing all the things that I needed to do to make that transition quickly. At the time, I was told I was the first woman to graduate from Rensselaer, who was both a full-time student and a single mom. I graduated with honors.

Education enabled me to move from being on the welfare rolls to living the life and having the career that I've had. Without education and some outstanding professors like Dr. Eric Gauger, and Dr. Barry Taylor, and many others, there's no way that I would be able to be here right now.

It's no different from my husband of 28 years. Because after I left my first husband, and after I graduated from Rensselaer, I married the man of my dreams. Marriage is a negotiated relationship. Our's was no different. We had a negotiated deal when we got married. I had three little kids, we were moving to new geography, And before we got married, we established the "terms and conditions" of our marriage. We talked parenting, finances, conflict, etc. Trust me; we missed a lot and found our philosophies changed over time. But, we started with an agreement about our what life would be as a married couple. I can tell you that 28 years later, while some of our negotiated deal's core elements are still intact, many things have changed. Our relationship has been renegotiated multiple times over the years.

## Negotiation As A Relationship

What makes me different and makes this book different is that we want to talk about negotiation, as that relationship.

We enter into business relationships, whether we formalize them in terms of a contract, or they're informal and written on the back of a napkin or sealed with a handshake. Often, we expect them to stay the same forever, but they don't. And we don't create opportunities that make it easy for each party in the relationship to renegotiate and set new terms and have that dialogue. Instead, we attach this negative emotion, almost shame, around the need to restructure a relationship.

We don't reward transparency the way we could, and we

don't approach it as a relationship; we approach it as a transaction. I'm passionate about helping people see that negotiation is about relationships. When I talk to people about negotiations, I see people physically react by clenching their fists and covering their entire body. They often say to me, "Oh my gosh, how can you talk about negotiation? It's so combative!"

That makes me so sad because it should not be that way, and it doesn't have to be that way. This book is different because I want to give small businesses power to embrace their business relationships, and make more out of them than they are today. I want them not to have to settle. I want small businesses to find ways to stand up for themselves, be strong in their negotiation, and find that power because they have more power than they think they do.

It's very much the case that anybody and any company can benefit from looking at relationships in a different way. One of the big things that people say today is, you want a customer for a lifetime. Any good salesperson will tell you that the best customer is the one they already have. However, when my clients say they believe in having a customer for a lifetime, I ask them, "What's your renegotiation strategy?" They look at me like I have five heads. They have no idea what I'm talking about. My response is, "Then you don't believe in having a customer for a lifetime."

If you don't have a renegotiation policy, you will not have a customer for a lifetime.

The same can be said about a marriage, a friendship, a partnership or a business. All relationships begin as a negotiation, they must be renegotiated.

# HOW TO USE THIS BOOK

W hile Harvard taught me a lot about the preparation aspects of negotiation, there were some things that I would challenge my professors on at times. And I came up with a different model based on my almost 30 years of experience negotiating across the globe. The model that I came up with is a three-circle Venn diagram. Hence, Venn Negotiation is my company name.

⁕

T he first circle is about Effective Preparation, knowing what you want, and why you want it. We're going to talk a lot about what that looks like.

The second circle is Successful Engagement. How you ask for what you want and how you communicate through that process will drive whether you can succeed in getting what you want. Because, if you ask it in a way that doesn't create goodwill, then you're not likely to achieve your objectives.

Then the third circle is about making sure you get what you want. It's really about making the deal work. And that happens through contracts. And it also includes having an opinion and an approach to renegotiation.

That's what we're going to cover in the book; those three circles that make up the Venn diagram.

⊛

P art I is Effective Preparation. You're going to learn how to negotiate in a way that makes you more confident in asking for what you want; you're going to learn the tools and techniques used by master negotiators and taught at Ivy League institutions. You're also going to be able to get more out of your negotiations.

T hen, in Part II, I'll share the elements of Successful Engagement. Negotiation is inherently emotional because people are emotional, period. The thing is, when you decide that you need something from somebody else, you immediately have an emotional connection to that want. Just the very function of wanting is emotional. Right?

That is, that's an emotional act. There's no way that you can get emotion out of a negotiation. You can make it so that the feelings are not negative, that they are not confrontational or aggressive. That said, negotiation is inherently emotional. Emotion comes into play in asking for what we want once we know what we want, why we want it, and how it translates to our counterpart. If it's doable for our counterpart, then the most challenging part is asking, and once we ask it, knowing what to ask for and knowing how to ask for it matters.

O nce we have this foundation in place, then we dive into Part III, Making the Deal Work. We are absolutely going to make this user friendly so that it doesn't scare people away, especially when we talk about that third circle of the Venn diagram, which includes the topic of contracts.

Usually, people shrink into the carpet's smallest fiber when I say that word. Often, the response I hear is - "What? Only attorneys deal with contracts!"

We're going to talk about a very simplistic way of understanding contracts because they're essential to business, and to life. 80% of a contract is business-related, not legal-related.

One of my goals is to help you, as a business owner, stop abdicating your business to your attorney who likely doesn't understand your business.

The objective of this book is to give you tools and techniques to engage in powerful negotiations that are a win-win for everybody involved.

Agreed? Let's begin.

# PART I

## EFFECTIVE PREPARATION

# 1

# KNOW WHAT YOU WANT

*Be clear in what you want,*
*down to the gnat's ass level details.*

L et's start by talking about knowing what you want and why you want it. The thing is, most people have some idea of what they want. We often talk about what we want in terms of demands. Usually, few spend the time necessary to fully define their wants and needs. Fewer still go a step further and think about what or how they will trade-off the less important things for the most important. It's important that we think about it in terms of tangible things. The problem with that is that many things that have value aren't necessarily tangible.

F or instance, you're going to buy a car. What are all the things that matter to you? If you're like most people, you'll think of the make and model, reliability, price, color, roof style, heated/cooled seats, and so on.

But, did you think to include when you wanted it?

Or are you willing to wait for it?

Timing is not necessarily a tangible thing; it's not necessarily something that we think about. But if you are a one-car household and your car was involved in an accident, the value of getting a car now may be higher to you. In fact, waiting for a car may have negative value for you because you need to get a rental, find others to drive you. Suppose you're going to want to drive it off the lot. In that case, you will negotiate differently than if you're putting down a deposit and waiting 12 months before you actually decide to buy it or not. Each has a different objective.

Do you want the floor model Ford F-150?

Or, are you willing to wait for a special order Tesla?

While we sometimes know some of the things that we want, we're often not clear about defining the whole of what we want. We've been conditioned to get down to brass tacks, boil things down to the bottom line. So, we frame our negotiations in terms of, "How much will this cost me?" And when we think about things in terms of cost, our brains automatically turn to the negative. We are now negotiating based on scarcity. It's no wonder so many people loathe the negotiation process. The feel they are going to lose something most of the time. We may think of things in terms of a price.

Many people say to me: "Oh, I don't negotiate because my prices aren't negotiable."

To those who believe they do not negotiate regularly, I ask - do you negotiate time?

Do you negotiate who owns what in terms of deliverables?

Do you negotiate bedtime with your kids?

Do you negotiate dinner plans with your spouse?

Do you negotiate vacation destinations with your friends?

There are many things that we negotiate. Being aware that you are in a negotiation is critical. Then, having clarity around what you want is hugely important.

When we're not clear in what we want, we cannot expect

others to understand. None of us are mind readers. We need to provide our counterparts with that clarity.

## LAYERING TO LEARN

Layering is effective and essential in clarifying what you want. It also contributes to making sure that what you're going to be asking of your counterpart is doable for your counterpart.

I'll use the example of when my husband and I wanted to buy our new cars. We walked into a dealership to buy two brand new Honda Elements, but we only wanted to pay for one of them.

We ended up buying two Honda Elements, paying for one of them, plus $5,000.

Considering that we saved $25,000 on the second Honda, the negotiation yielded a successful outcome for us as well as for the dealership.

We couldn't have done that without being clear about what we wanted from the negotiation in the first place. While we didn't achieve the initial goal, we were able to achieve a negotiation that suited us.

We did that in part by layering. The first part of the process was for me to sit down with my husband and confirm what we will want out of a car. My husband really loved the Honda Element. I was not as excited as he was about that car, so I didn't care about the outcome.

My husband and I are campers. For that, the Element was great because we could hose out the car after a camping trip.

Also, we drive manual transmissions. We are old-school drivers and love the power and control we get with a manual transmission. We knew that we wanted a sunroof, and we knew what we could pay. We knew what we wanted.

We wrote a list of the things we want.

Then we established the order of importance - how vital were those things?

Why did we want those things?

What were we willing to give up on?

That became an essential aspect of our layering because it helped us determine what our trade-offs were. After all, his car had been in an accident. We needed to drive off the lot with a car, at least one, because we really didn't need two vehicles. We just needed to get one, but we knew we wanted to drive off the lot with the car. We knew what we wanted; we knew why we wanted it. Then we had to figure out whether or not it was doable for the car dealer.

I did a great deal of research. I researched what the market was for the Honda Element. What were the competitive cars on the market?

Who was their target market?

What percentage of drivers in New England, where we lived at the time, drove manual transmissions?

It was something like 7%.

The target market age-range for the Honda Element was under 30.

There were a lot fewer people under the age of 30 that knew how to drive a manual transmission.

We found a website that told us how many of these cars sat on the lots of different dealers in our area. We found the dealer who had the most manual transmission Honda Elements on their lot, and they had four of them.

It was the second Friday of January. Many people will tell you it is a terrible time to buy a car because they're just coming off their holiday boom, and they're not really in the mood to make a deal.

I gave my husband a role, and I had my part.

We went in with all this information, and I was able to make a deal through layering because we understood what we wanted and why we wanted it. We knew what we were able to give up and our trade-offs, how the business of car selling worked, and what the market was for this product. We were able to secure a deal where we drove off the lot that night in two brand new Honda Elements.

We paid for one plus $5,000 for the second because of the inventory holding costs for the dealership. We adjusted the deal. We felt good about the deal, and the dealership did too.

My husband and I took those two Honda Elements on many camping trips together over the years.


## ORDER OF MAGNITUDE

For those who hate researching and are entirely averse to doing research, remember that an hour to two hours of research on the Honda Element and how car dealers sell cars saved me $25,000.

It was worth the one to two hours of research to do that. The other thing to keep in mind is that negotiation is not about precision. It's not about perfection. It's about the order of magnitude.

You don't need to go to super detailed levels in many negotiations. There are times if it's a very complex negotiation with many parties when you need to get to very, very detailed numbers. But for most businesses, negotiation is more about getting to an order of magnitude. It's not about precision.

You absolutely need to set priorities in big-picture terms.

Order of magnitude means I'm not negotiating with the penny. I'm negotiating to the $10, or the hundred dollars. I'm not going to quibble over tiny, tiny amounts when it doesn't add much value. I'll negotiate for $1,000, not $1.99. You have to determine your own order of magnitude. For some, it's $1, others $1,000, others $100,000, and still others even a $1 million.


## EXPANDING YOUR INTERPRETATIONS

It's crucial that you don't negotiate against yourself before you've even engaged with your counterpart, and many of us do that.

In the example of buying two cars for the price of one, I'm going to ask you, would you have ever thought to go to a dealership and ask to buy two cars for the price of one?

I'm confident that for the vast majority of you, the answer is no.

Some of you might say, "Oh, I'll go to a dealer and try to get two cars for the price of one, just to see if I can do it."

The reality is that's not how or why we did that. We did it based on what we figured out was doable for the dealer. We knew that the dealer in that situation was not injured. We were not annihilating them; we were not causing them any harm. We weren't causing the salesperson any damage by going in and asking that. The request was doable. That became important.

But, if I had told somebody ahead of time that I was going to try to buy two cars, for the price of one, people would have said, "You're out of your mind." Then I would have convinced myself that I couldn't do it.

Throughout history, there are many examples where somebody did something they thought was impossible, like the first person to break the four-minute mile. Then everyone started breaking the four-minute mile.

Not that everyone's going to be able to go out and buy two cars for the price of one, but you know it's possible now.

Now you have a new anchor in your mind that says, "Oh, I can do that, I never thought about being able to do that."

Not many of you are probably going to try to do it, but it's still doable. Think about a negotiation that you're entering. Now, think about the improbable things you want.

Use the exercise to expand your thinking. Allow yourself to think differently. Give yourself permission to think bigger. I do this for every deal I do and then I write down those ideas. It is a powerful exercise that allows me to confront and overcome the doubt in my own mind.

Imagine you have decided to go after a different type of

customer. Close your eyes and think about who that customer might be. What do they want?

Now let's think about it. If it's a supplier and you want a new supplier, you want to improve your service quality to your customers. You want to lower your costs.

What does that look like?

What does that relationship look like?

How fast are you getting product?

Who's holding inventory?

What matters in terms of the relationship with them?

Are you able to get good customer service?

Do you have remedies if the customer service isn't what it should be?

What type of customer service experience do you want to have?

What do you want your relationship to be with the supplier's salesperson or team?

How fast do you want to get product?

If it's a product, how do you want inventory to managed?

Do you have remedies if customer service isn't what was agreed?


L et's say that you work for somebody else.

What is that job?

What do you get for vacation?

Do you have a 401k?

Do you have insurance?

What kind of salary do you think is important to you?

Take a sheet of paper and write all that and more down. Just let things flow from your mind to your pen to your paper. Avoid censuring yourself. Give yourself permission to explore all the possibilities you can imagine. When you do that, you'll start to see that you actually want, more than you may be willing to ask for. You may just experience an awakening.

## SELF-NEGOTIATION

That awakening that you just had is absolutely the first step of negotiating with ourselves. We often convince ourselves that we can't ask for something. We can't ask for two cars for the price of one, or the job with a 25% salary increase, and a down-payment for a house. We can't get that big customer and still maintain our profitability, or a good supplier who will be with us through thick and thin. We won't be able to ensure that we continue to treat our customers in the right way. But you can. You can get more of what you want.

After having done the exercise, some of you may have discovered that you've actually asked for less than what you really wanted. You told yourself it wasn't possible and you believed it before even asking. This happens a lot.

I spoke with a venture capitalist the other week, who told me that often people come in seeking funding for their business idea. They have a great business idea, but they don't ask for even as much as they need to make the business viable, let alone what they want to make it successful. That means that they're putting their business at risk by not asking for what they want. When you ask for just what you need, you're likely going to get negotiated down. It's essential to get yourself to that 'want' state and figure out how to get more of that.

When you're starting below your needs, you have to figure out the steps, whether you can take a big step or take incremental steps to move closer to what you want.

.  .  .

I f you're somebody who's operating below your floor, you've sacrificed your needs. You may need to reacquaint yourself with what those needs are so you can start to move toward them before you can even get yourself to wrap your head around what your wants are.

First, you need to articulate what those needs are. When I talk about job negotiations with people, I encourage people to write out their budget. Your need is your budget. It is the bare minimum that allows you to pay your bills and eat and have a roof over your head every month. That's your base need. Sometimes a job discussion is the easiest way to explain that.

I t's true for an entrepreneur as well. What's the bare minimum you need to make to keep yourself and your business afloat? If you're not afloat, your business isn't working either. Once you figure that out, you've got to figure out what your steps are that you're going to do and take to get to that floor. Once you're there, you can start to think more about your wants, but you've got to overcome that gap. When you are not even meeting your basic needs, your ability to think, in terms of self-actualization, of your wants, is much harder to do.

## THE FORMULA FOR NEGOTIATION

If you're not getting your needs met, one of the tools that I have found useful is using objective data to help me articulate what the need is. I certainly used this tool when I was not getting my needs met when I was on welfare and figuring things out.

As a general rule, we prefer to see people meeting their needs. It's very distressing to see somebody who's not able to meet their needs. Having a clear view of data permitted me to ask to make sure my needs were getting met when I was not in a state where I could start thinking about what I wanted. I was only thinking about what my bare minimum needs were. Having that objective data helped make it easier for me to ask for my needs because then it wasn't just an emotional ask; it was a fact-based ask.

I knew that I had to pay this much in rent. I knew I had to pay this much for food, whatever was in my budget. When I got my first job offer out of Rensselaer, I knew exactly what that need was, right? I turned down some job offers because they didn't meet that need. It made it much easier for me to do that. I found comfort in the numbers to help me get there.

The research will help you in many ways. It will help you clarify your objectives and create non-emotional ways of connecting with what those needs are. Once your needs are met, you can use that same approach to justify and explain your wants.

Because, in business, every company has to make a margin. If you're a company that's going to be around for a long time, and that's your goal, you need to make a margin. You need to have an idea of what that margin is going to look like. Once you have an idea of that margin, you need to base that on top of your needs. You're trying to get to that margin so you can have a sustainable business that will grow. Your customers want you to be a business that will grow because people don't like to change whom they buy things from. In fact, some studies suggest that you, as a supplier, could raise your price almost 40% before somebody changes suppliers.

That tells you how much people do not like to change their suppliers. When you know that, you can build and build your margin into things and start to sustain yourself more.

. . .

I want to make it clear, in the short time we've been together, how important research, numbers, and sitting down with a piece of paper is. How much of a difference it makes and how important it is. You can control your emotions more effectively when you've got the research and data in front of you. Remember, negotiation is inherently emotional. That whole act of wanting something we talked about earlier. However, letting your emotions take over the negotiation will guarantee a poor outcome for everyone, but especially for you.

For the negotiation to not pull you in emotionally, you must be clear on your numbers before engaging with your counterpart.

## KNOW YOUR NUMBERS

It's critical that you understand your numbers before engaging with your counterpart.

I'll use the example of a company I helped negotiate a software deal. They were buying 600 concurrent licenses a year, which meant that more than one person could be accessing the software simultaneously, up to 600 people. It was costly software, roughly $10,000 a year per license, plus support and maintenance fees of 21%. An annual cost of $7.26 million for each year of the 5 year contract. A grand total of $36.3 million.

It was a huge investment.

The first thing that I did with my team was to question;

Who was using the software?

What were they using it for?

How were they using it?

How often were they using it?

How often does this group use it relative to that group?

When were they using it at the same time?

We went through this whole analysis to understand exactly

how this product was being used and operated in the client. We found that they were only using 280 licenses a year, but they were paying for 600 licenses a year. Now, there was one week a year in which they went over 400 licenses. They were not using all 600.

It would have been less expensive for them to get 300 licenses and pay the penalty for going up over 400 for that one week, a year. We successfully negotiated a reduction in the number of licenses. We successfully reduced the number of licenses and lowered the maintenance fee to 18%. By understanding what, where, when, and how our client was using the software, we were able to save our client $12.7 million.

They had been buying the software for years. They wasted millions of dollars because internally, they did not understand how they used it, when they used it, and what they used it for. They thought that it was being used in a completely different way, but nobody had bothered to do the analysis. If you don't understand your numbers, you cannot truly understand their impact on your business when you go into a negotiation. It's one of the reasons why I frustrate procurement people, sometimes quite a bit. I won't negotiate price until we've finished negotiating the contract. Within the contract, there are a lot of different aspects that drive the profitability of that relationship. Those aspects could be insurance rates, payment terms, inventory holding, customer service, or product quality issues; all of those things drive cost.

If somebody comes to me saying, "Well, you can buy this product at x price," my response is , "That doesn't mean anything to me at this point in time."

I need to take the deal and evaluate it against my financials to make sure that the deal works. When you put price first, you're incurring costs related to the deal that don't necessarily make sense.

My team's inquiry saved that company $2.5 million a year. It took some time and research, but it was well worth the time it took documenting, researching, and learning.

It might be easy to assume that it took a long time for my team to do that. The thing that can be challenging is that, on my end, when I look at businesses, it is that many times this stuff doesn't take that much time.

But, it's well worth it.

It's just that we get busy, wrapped up in our day to day, and we make choices not to do it, or we trust people at their word, and we don't verify it. Then we must live with decisions that don't have the best outcomes, and we end up with ineffective deals.

Hopefully, you have a greater appreciation for the importance of information and preparation in your negotiation.

# 2

# NEGOTIATION WITH YOUR INNER CRITIC

*The hardest part of any negotiation
happens between your ears.*

How do you react emotionally when you're in that process of negotiating against ourselves? Where your heart is saying that this is what you want, but your head is saying, "Oh, no, no, no. That's too high risk! You can't ask for that."

Your mind will convince you that they're going to hate you, they're going to think you're a fool or an idiot, you're asking too much, you're not worth this, maybe so and so could get this, but you certainly can't get that. You believe that you're not qualified enough.

Whatever that 'I'm not' kind of language is, it's because our subconscious mind is trying to protect us. It's all about that protection mode and making sure that we don't put ourselves in danger. It really likes to keep things that status quo. Your brain spends an inordinate amount of time talking you out of doing things that would put you in a better position because it's all nice and warm and cozy, right where it is.

When I was training for my black belt in martial arts, one of my instructors once explained that, when it comes to making changes in our lives, people are kind of screwed. Why? Because the human being consists mainly of water and electricity. Water seeks its lowest level, and electricity seeks the path of least resistance. When we're trying to climb out of something, we are going against physics that work to keep us down.

What ends up happening is that people who are down in the hole with us, they see us start to climb, but they're not climbing. That makes them feel inadequate and makes them feel "less than".

So, instead of rising with you, they try to pull you down.

For me, I was able to be tenacious because I had people around me who kept helping to pull me up. Whenever I started to go back down again, they were there, pulling me up. That includes my children, who were the ages of three, four, and five when I was at Rensselaer. My oldest daughter ultimately sacrificed a lot of her childhood so that I could go to school and find a better way of being a mom and providing a better life for them. It really was my whole family that helped make everything possible.

A great example is that my husband just changed jobs. He'd started working for a company about ten years ago, and it was the company of his dreams. He loved it. Then it was purchased by a big company a few years ago. Now he took the job in 2010, and the market hadn't improved since the 2008 crash. His salary was not what he wanted to be. He took a $60,000 a year pay cut because he had lost his job and had been unemployed for several months, and he never made it up at that company. When he decided that he wanted to get a new job, I said, you need to write down that your new job would pay you at the same rate you would have been paid, had you kept at your salary, in your last position.

And he got it.

His salary increased over 25% with one job move, though he spent a lot of time telling himself and me that it would never happen. He was convinced, there was no way it can happen.

That happened in July of 2020, in the middle of the pandemic. He got a new job with a 25% plus salary increase, and many other things that were important to him in his negotiation. His own head voices kept telling him it wasn't doable, and I was there saying this is absolutely doable. It's totally possible. Finally, he believed it, and when they asked him how much his salary expectation was. He told them, they agreed. It's as easy as that.

## THE MUST-HAVES TO WIN

There are three essential ingredients for successful negotiations: people, clarity, and action.

Surround yourself with supportive people. Those are your cheerleaders that very much have the mindset to celebrate your wins.

They see you, appreciate you, and value you for who you are today, in this moment. They are not trying to mold you into someone else. Nor are the focused on your potential. They are focused on you. Vision Coach, Carey Conley, often asks, "Who is in the front row of your life?" Are they your biggest support-ers, people who love you so much they challenge you to be even better? People who celebrate your wins and guide you through the losses? Because if they aren't those people, you should, as Carey says, move them to the balcony. I add you may need to move them to the nose-bleed seats. There will always be times when you doubt yourself. We all do. Make sure you're surrounded by people whose belief in you never waivers because you'll need to lean on them when you don't have enough belief in yourself.

Second, you must get clarity on what you want, which we discussed earlier.

To get clarity, you must have a process.

Then, you must take definitive action to implement that process with your people.

## CLARITY OF ASSUMPTIONS

Get people to negotiate the assumptions first. Don't talk numbers. Talk about the assumptions used to get to the numbers. Once people agree to the assumptions, it's harder to argue about the output. The assumptions that go into the math, then the numbers coming out of it, that's just the math, but you agreed to all the assumptions. So, getting clarity on that and building around that is hugely, hugely valuable.

With the Honda Elements example, the assumption was that the dealer was losing money by having four manual transmission cars on the lot. The problem and hypothesis were that there were a small number of under 30-year-old manual transmission driving buyers in the market to buy that vehicle. Therefore, they would have had to do something different with that car, and it would be better for them to move that car off the lot. That was an assumption going into that. When we were in the negotiation with the dealer, we said that this was the assumption. The dealer corrected us on our hypotheses. It wasn't quite the right assumption.

The dealer updated my hypothesis by providing me new, verifiable data, which got us to a different number. But it was the assumption that drove the conversation, not the number itself.

I crafted a theory, tested it with external data, and knew the source of my data. If I hadn't done that, I would have accepted any data the dealership provide without verifying it. Because I had my data and shared it when asked, we could negotiate with greater clarity and understanding.

In Chapter 3, I'll share more strategies and other types of things that you can do to help you step into your power.

## SUPPORT SYSTEM

It's essential that you surround yourself with people who will help you be the best you. One of the things we're going to talk about more in the program is that the most significant part of negotiation is the negotiation that happens between our ears, the negotiation that we have with ourselves.

When we're trying to get something from a counterpart, we cannot effectively do that if we don't believe in our heart of hearts, deep within ourselves, that we're worthy of it and that we're deserving of it. Because, when we don't believe that we're worthy of it or are deserving of it, we start negotiating against ourselves, often before we even engage with a counterpart. Belief in yourself is crucial, as is surrounding yourself with supportive people who will challenge you in a caring way. As previously mentioned, those people will be critical for your long-term success and as a negotiator and just as a human being.

So far, we've been talking in terms of negotiation with ourselves.

When we don't see our own value, we dive to the minimum. Once we permit ourselves to feel that we are adding value, we start talking more about wants and desires. Your hopes and dreams.

You get feedback from others that you're doing a good job, and you begin to see it. Then it becomes easier.

There's a reason why people who have been wildly successful financially and then gone completely and utterly bankrupt can quickly rebuild their wealth. They have a new expectation. They have a new minimum. Their expectations are higher. They did it once. They can do it again. They expect it to be there for them. As Maya Angelou said: "Ask for what you want and be prepared to get it."

What you were doing in that process was building a new baseline, every time you got a higher salary, you were changing your baseline. When you're accustomed to making $100,000 a year, you're not likely to accept a job, except in extremely unusual conditions, for less than $100,000 a year. Your base requirement is different, and your needs are different, so your expectations have increased.

Unless somebody comes to you and says; "Oh, you were doing a great job," you often forget the value that you are adding to a situation.

Even in my own story, recently, I've been negotiating a real estate lease for a couple of clients. It hasn't gone quite the way that I wanted it to, which is frustrating me.

There are many circumstances around this particular situation. But then, I talked to an expert in the commercial real estate profession. I explained the deal that I had to negotiate, and he responded along the lines of - "Are you kidding? That's crazy! Nobody's getting that kind of a deal."

Suddenly, instead of being frustrated with the situation, I began thinking about different ways I might have approached the deal.

We don't always know the value we're creating. Getting external confirmation that you're adding value and getting evidence for yourself that you're adding value becomes an essential part of your contribution to the negotiation. Then you have a new point of conversation about this particular situation. Now it's not about you as a whole. It's about a situation. And once you have that change in mentality, it changes how you approach your conversations going forward.

## ACCOMPLISHMENT JOURNAL

Many business coaches in the personal development space advocate that as an employee or an entrepreneur, it's beneficial to make value lists of what you bring to the table.

I've not made value lists. It depends on your personality. If you're somebody who is motivated by seeing something in writing, you should absolutely do that.

Instead, I advocate that you keep an Accomplishments Journal. That's more practical for me. Daily, I write down what I accomplished today, and let me tell you; there are some days when I got out of bed and brushed my teeth. There have been those days over the years when that was a significant accomplishment. But, then there are days when I've closed billion-dollar deals that are on that list. And over time, what happens is, when I'm not in a positive place, I can go back and look at that Accomplishments Journal. I look at all the fantastic things that I have done.

The value list is somewhat similar in that you keep track of the value you've added to the relationship or relationships. You track that, and you have a way of monitoring that. I prefer to do that through testimonials. When people tell me that I've done a great job, I'll keep track of that information as a way of tracking my value. I think of that as a more powerful way of doing it. Then it's somebody else's words and not just my own. It gives me an external voice. When I do not feel that I add value, then I have another external voice saying, "No, you're adding a great deal of value. And this is where you did it and how you did it and why that's amazing."

## TESTIMONIALS

I am working at converting everything to video testimonials because they're just more powerful. In today's environment, video carries a lot more weight than a written testimonial. And there's a question about credibility with some written testimonials. If you're going to do a written testimonial, try to have a photo. Use the person's name and picture because people question the validity of testimonials these days (because of bots and all that stuff). It is paramount to confirm that it's a real human being who actually said that to you.

Be careful with painting your business with only glowing testimonials. I had a situation not long ago where I'd engaged a "branding expert" I'd met at a conference to do some work for me. I was very dissatisfied with the outcome. He commented to me that he'd been in business for over ten years. He told me that he'd never had a bad customer service experience. I said to him, "If you've been in business for over ten years; and never had single complaint, you're lying."

The probability of 100% of his customers being 100% satisfied after more than ten years of business is negligible. It's not impossible, but it is improbable that he didn't have at least some customer service issues. The thing was, he just didn't have a process for dealing with them. That was an issue that he needed to figure out, and I got all my money back from that situation.

His initial position was that he didn't believe me because I have all these great customer testimonials.

My response was that just because you have all these great customer testimonials does not mean you don't have any bad ones. It just means that you have hidden them. Or, you don't have a system or a framework to receive critical feedback.

I would absolutely encourage people to make use of the Accomplishments Journals and Testimonials as a way of keeping track of your value. But don't forget that those are still subjective points; those are biased pieces of evidence. Fact-based evidence will help bolster whatever position you have that you can substantiate through your testimonials. Through data and analysis, you can verify your accomplishments in an Accomplishments Journal. The two must be together. One without the other is not nearly as effective. If all you have are testimonials and what people say and do not provide a depth of facts and data.

# 3

# BEGIN WITH WHY

*Treat price as an output to your negotiation,
not the input.*

T he 'why' you want something is essential because it drives your trade-offs. Whenever we're negotiating, it's common to have multiple things that we want. You may want insurance, a 401k, a certain amount of vacation time, plus your salary in a job negotiation. If you are negotiating for a car, like my Honda Element story, you may want a manual transmission, a sunroof, this, that, and the other thing. If you're in a business, you want certain things. There are usually multiple things that you want in a negotiation.

Suppose you're negotiating for just one thing. Say you're at an antique market, and you're bargaining to buy a rug. In that case, you're probably haggling more than you're negotiating because you're focused on one specific thing; getting a rug for a certain price. Haggling is different than negotiating.

In a negotiation, there are usually multiple variables that you're looking for. But, they're not all equally important. Usually, you'll give something of lesser value away for something more consequential. Because something unimportant to you could be important to your counterpart. You want to know what you want and why you want it and why it's important to you. Because, if you don't understand that 'why' component, you may inadvertently give something away that's important to you, but not to your counterpart, and you don't want to do that. You want to try to make sure that you're giving away the less important things in exchange for getting the essential things. If you don't understand why something is important to you, you'll lose focus on what your ultimate goal is in your negotiation. Then you're not going to be as successful in your negotiation process as you'd like to be.

## THE WHAT AND WHY EXERCISE

I want to take you through an exercise to understand your 'what' and your 'why.' It's pretty simplistic but shocking how few people do this for their negotiation. Earlier, we talked about opening your mind to the possibilities. We did that visioning exercise to avoid negotiating against yourself before you even engage with a counterpart.

Now you know that there are greater possibilities in terms of what you're going to ask for.

The first step is to make a list. It can be on a piece of paper, a spreadsheet, open a document, and write down what you want from the negotiation. I'm talking about every possible thing you can think of. It should be a fairly exhaustive list, and it's going to be entirely dependent on what you're negotiating. In gross terms, you're going to have things around price; you will have some things around the product quality, your service quality, and those things that are specific to the situation. You're going to have some big buckets. Still, you want to get specific because the specifics will matter as you go through the dialogue with your counterpart.

Once you've got that list of all the things you want in this negotiation, you want to evaluate and prioritize them.

How important are they?

Why are they important?

What about that particular thing is important to you?

What happens if you don't get that thing?

Is it the end of the world? Do you lose 50% of your margin?

Does it create issues with your staff?

Do you need to have new resources?

What are those things?

Why?

That helps you set your prioritization. The things that are at the bottom of the list are those that you can give up. You may give them up to make sure you get those three or five big things that are going to drive the most significant amount of value in the negotiation.

## PRIORITIZATION LIST

This is the most critical element to this exercise. Now keep in mind, you have not engaged with our counterpart yet—everything you're doing at this point you are basing on assumptions. Even on your list, you assume that something is more important, but you still have to be open when you engage with your counterpart, which I'm going to talk about in Part II.

Once you engage in work with your counterpart, they might offer something that has even more value than what you have on your list. One of the big things about negotiation is being open to that possibility. Before going into talks, you want to have an idea of what you want. Know all of the things you want and why they're significant. Then set those prioritizations to figure out the most important things.

## BE PREPARED

This is the most crucial section of all of them. Preparedness is something that very few people do before going into a negotiation.

When you go into a negotiation unprepared, you will almost certainly be unhappy with the end result. At a minimum, you just don't get the results you wanted as often as you could. You don't get as much of what you want, as much as you could be getting, because you haven't prepared enough. We've talked about knowing how important it is to define what it is that you want. We've talked about getting out of your own head and not negotiating against yourself by creating more substantial possibilities. We've talked about knowing that while it may seem impossible or improbable to get it. If there is a probability that you can get it, you should ask for it anyway.

We've talked about the importance of knowing why you have something on your negotiation list—prioritizing that so you can understand your trade-offs. We've talked about why it's vital to grasp how what you want will impact your counterpart. You need to figure out if something is doable. Ask.

Is it possible to buy two cars for the price of one?

Or, is that completely impossible to do?

Preparation helps you figure out the world of the possible. In negotiation, in my many years of experience doing it, more things are possible than impossible.

I have a saying - *if you can conceive it, you can paper it.*

If you can think about it, and it comes to your mind, you can find a way to get that into a contract and make it real, as long as it's legal.

This is how you make the impossible, possible.

# PART II

SUCCESSFUL ENGAGEMENT

# 4

# ON THE ELEMENTS OF A
# SUCCESSFUL ENGAGEMENT

*Most contractual risk has nothing to do with the law. It's about your business.*

Now that we've completed the first segment, the preparation, we're going into successful engagement, which is the second of the three keys. In this section, we're going to talk about the elements of a successful engagement, which begins with the initiation of the conversation. That's where it gets juicy. You are now engaging; this is the fun part.

The first part of engagement is initiating the conversation, where knowing your communication attributes becomes important. It is the first place where you're able to start to build goodwill and get small successes. That is, you've done your research, and you know with whom you're negotiating. Now you're going to reach out to them, either by email, or phone, or text, and start to engage in that conversation.

Suppose you are somebody like me, who gets hired to negotiate. In that case, you may want somebody to make that introduction to your counterpart for you. I often have my clients introduce me to my counterpart. Still, there are times when I want to take my counterpart a bit by surprise, particularly if my counterpart is behaving like a Champion to my clients. Then I often will take on a little bit more of a Champion role, just so that they know that I'm not an easy pushover and somebody they will have to deal with. There are several things that you want to do when you initiate the conversation. Because you're adapting initially to their communication attribute, let's just assume that you're building goodwill by making that adaptation to their style, whether or not it matches yours.

The other thing you want to make sure you do is to start the conversation about the process. You want to explain why you are in the negotiation. What is it about this individual that you want to engage them for?

In my case, it's usually because my clients have asked me to engage with them, which always creates many questions for the counterpart. Sometimes the counterpart may wonder why my clients aren't talking for themselves. They get suspicious as to why I am speaking on my client's behalf. That's a question that I need to answer, and I work with my clients to figure out what that answer is before I speak with their counterpart. If you're renegotiating a deal that already exists, then you need to be able to have a justification. We will discuss the motives for engaging in a renegotiation later in the book. For now, we're just talking about a good old-fashioned negotiation, you don't have a relationship with this person, but they have something that you want.

You've communicated with them to set up a call or a meeting, you're going to adapt it according to their communication attribute. The next thing is trying to agree on how this negotiation process will unfold because that is important.

When people think about negotiation, many believe negotiation equals sales. It does not mean that sales aren't a part of the negotiation, but it is not the whole of the negotiation. Sales often focus just on price and don't focus on the other things that drive price. Frequently, when I've worked in sales and sales departments, I've taught people how to negotiate. One of the first things that I tell people to do is, make sure you have clarity on the negotiation process.

Who is involved in it?

How long is it?

How long does it take to get approvals?

Who signs the contract?

All these different elements are part of the process.

⚜

## DAVID AND GOLIATH

In a David and Goliath negotiation, Goliath usually says: "This is my process. Therefore, you will live with that."

Do not assume that you must live with their process. You are a smaller business and can act more quickly and nimbly to figure out ways to accelerate different aspects of the deal.

Make sure that you get some elements of your process woven into the negotiation process. It's a way for you to set up both credibility and it acknowledges how important the relationship is to you.

Still, also to assert your voice in the negotiation to say, "I'm not just going to live with what you tell me I have to do; I have a say in this as well."

That process will dictate when you get revenue in or when you can start to get product in, and you want to contribute to that. That's one of the enormous things when you're initiating the conversation: to figure out what that process will be.

Once you get an agreement on that process, you both have a win in that column; you have reached an amicable agreement on what this process will be. That can set the tone for the rest of the negotiation. You now have something tangible that you can continue to build on as you move through the negotiation process.

When Goliath, the giant corporation, says, "this is the way we do things," you can tactfully assert yourself by saying, "this is how I'm going to do it." They have to be somewhat malleable, that makes them respect you a little bit more.

Putting your stamp on the process, even in a small way, elevates you and gives you more credibility. You are showing leadership by not agreeing to follow just their process. It doesn't have to be significant changes. A big company has very explicit processes that they go through to get agreements negotiated and signed off on before anyone can issue purchase orders, and that's an exacting process.

You want to make sure that in that process, you're making sure that you have a step in it that's labeled and written out. It can even be a minor clause - as the owner, you have to sign off here, or need to have a certain aspect vetted.

In part of your process, if you're a small business owner, usually you are where the buck stops. Be careful with that because one of the benefits of a larger organization is that you have a hierarchy of approval, and approvals matter in the negotiation process. Having somebody who isn't the final decision maker negotiating is powerful because you have somebody who can escalate the deal to you for final approval.

But, if you're negotiating as the business owner, you have nobody to whom you can escalate the agreement. That puts you in a potentially dangerous position because you are more likely to get emotionally involved in that negotiation versus being a little bit away from the negotiation. That's one of the benefits that a big company has is this approval process.

It's potent to say in a negotiation that the board is going to have to sign off on that. Boards don't meet every week. So that adds much time to the negotiation process. If you can insert that stamp of yours on that negotiation process, it means that you have more credibility.

## THE ADVISORY BOARD

To be clear, if you don't have a board, do not ever say that you have somebody else who has to sign off on the decision. The number one rule in negotiation is: do not lie.

Now you can talk around many things, and you can speak around being bluntly factual. You can still answer a question without answering it altogether, just never lie.

If you do not have a board, do not say that you will need the board's approval. If you don't have a board, I'd recommend that you get a group of advisors and set up an advisory board. If you have an advisory board, you might not say I need to get my board's approval; you might say I need to get my board's recommendations. You are not asking for permission because they're an advisory board, not a formal board of directors; the decision still sits with you. In Chapter 7, I give you the details for how to create your first advisory board.

Perhaps, as part of your agreement with your advisory board, you should discuss crucial decisions such as bringing on new big customers or big suppliers with your advisory board before acting on it. I would encourage you to have an advisory board that you can at least say, I need to talk to get my board's recommendations on this.

## THE HEAD NOD

As a general rule, I am what I affectionately call a head-nodder at the negotiation table, the Zoom room, or the Teams meeting, depending on where I am.

People will talk, and they'll put proposals on the table, and I nod my head because I'm listening very carefully. We'll talk about listening with intent in greater detail in Chapter 6. Intentional listening is hugely important. I'm listening to the words that are coming out of my counterpart's mouth.

But, it does not necessarily mean I agree with those words. I will tell people that I do that because, in certain cultures, head-nodding implies agreement. I will let people know that I sit and nod my head in the affirmative, that I'm listening to them, but not that I am agreeing with them. I'll let people know that is how I behave in a negotiation. I'm listening with intent. I don't necessarily acquiesce to things at the table unless I've already decided that I could agree to them before I got into that meeting. If I have had that dialogue and discussion and made that analysis and come to that conclusion. Before that meeting, if it is something new, I will take it and evaluate it offline, on my own.

⊛

The book: *Getting to Yes*, written by Roger Fisher and William Ury, is one of the vanguard books for creating the whole negotiation industry. They talk about "going to the balcony."

*Going to the balcony* is when you have something that comes up, and you don't fully understand it, or there is too much tension. Things get heated, voices get raised, and you're not able to agree, you go to the balcony, and you take a break. Sometimes the recess can be five minutes, and sometimes it can go on for five days; it depends on the negotiation. Sometimes it can be even longer than that. It depends entirely on the negotiation. That is an essential tool to use because you want to be thoughtful and intentional about the conversation that you're having and what you are negotiating.

This can be minimized, as we talked about in Chapter 1, if

you have followed the elements of preparation. The thing about preparation is it is all about you, even the parts when you're thinking about how this deal could impact your counterpart. You're still thinking about what you want and what you need to succeed in that deal. All you have about your counterpart are assumptions. That whole section, where we talked about understanding the impact of what you want on your counterpart, those are assumptions. You have done research and homework, and now you're at the table. And guess what? You are not the most important person at the table. You know everything there is to know right now about you and what you want, all you have are assumptions.

You have a hypothesis about what the deal means to your counterpart, and your time at the table should always be about figuring out whether your expectations are accurate or not. If they're not, you can adjust them.

## TAKE YOUR TIME

*Time is a strategic resource.*

Suppose a new negotiation item comes to the table that you didn't anticipate. In that case, you shouldn't decide right then and there, because it is new information. You need it to ruminate and digest a bit, percolate. So, it's best if you step away, for whatever time-period might be suitable, and then revisit with a little bit more clarity.

My recommendation is typically, especially if it's an essential element, to take a step away from the discussion and evaluate. Go back to your analysis to decide if it still fits, which may take you one minute or two minutes; it could take you longer. Make sure you are affording yourself the time to evaluate it. It is better to take that time and be thoughtful about it than to make a knee jerk reaction, react to it, agree to it, or even reject it. Either way, you could be committing yourself to a decision that may not be in your best interest if you decide at that moment. You don't know, and you're guessing at that time, so my recommendation is to take that step back.

There are several different types of indicators for you to know when the right time to return to the negotiation table is.

The first one is to listen to your gut. I know that some people might say, "Oh, Christine, that's a little woo-woo."

But really, part of it is paying attention to what your gut is telling you. If it doesn't feel right, then there's something not right about it. You just don't know what it is yet. You've got to trust that instinct.

In Malcolm Gladwell's book, *Blink*, he talks a lot about how we see something and know it's wrong. We say there's something not right, but we can't put our finger on it, so we dismiss it. Then guess what? It comes back and bites us, and we think, "Dang it, I knew something wasn't right. I shouldn't have dismissed that."

I'm working with some individuals right now who entered into a negotiation. When they first negotiated a deal, they kind of got screwed on the deal, so we're trying to renegotiate it. However, when they went into the negotiation, the counterpart was kind of a jerk. He was one of those bully kinds of guys. In their gut, they knew it didn't feel right; they felt that they don't want to do business like this. But they came up with all these rationales and justifications as to why they should do business with this guy. They wish that they hadn't done it because their gut-feeling has become a reality. Now, they are tens of thousands of dollars out of money. They have to figure out how to unwind the negotiation.

One is just listening to that gut thing, again, because negotiation is inherently emotional. People are intrinsically emotional; that emotion is a real thing. It's a decent way of taking the temperature on something. Still, not every aspect of negotiation will elicit that kind of gut response. The things that are most emotional in the negotiation could trigger some type of gut reaction. Something that is not very important to us is not likely to do that. It doesn't mean that they're less important to evaluate in the negotiation; it just means we're not as emotionally attached to the outcome of that particular part of the negotiation.

## THE POWER OF NO

*Except in sex, no is an invitation to
ask a different question.*

No is a fantastic word. And guess what? It's also a full stop sentence with two letters.

When my kids were little, I don't know how many times I used to say to them, "Is it the N, the O, or the full sentence you don't understand?"

What about that short little word that is a sentence is challenging?

I love David and Goliath negotiations. I get much joy out of those negotiations' outcomes when I can help my clients achieve something that they never thought was possible in that kind of a deal. They walk away, going, "Oh, my gosh, this is just incredible." It just feels excellent when that happens. One of the ways of setting that up is knowing when no is the right answer.

I was negotiating a deal with a well-known telecommunications company; my client wasn't a small company, but it wasn't a large company. We were in the negotiation, and the telecommunications company came back to me with a condition. They wanted a full 80% discount instead of the 50 to 60% discount they were already getting. I don't negotiate price upfront; I wait to negotiate price till I have all the other costs driving aspects of the deal negotiated. At the end of the negotiation he said, "Well, we want 80%."

He shot this to me in an email. I hit reply and said, "no." There was nothing else.

He said it as a declarative sentence, "We want an 80% discount." He was not going to get that. We would have lost our shirts on that kind of a deal. There was no rationale for it.

My next response was, "Under what conditions do you think that we would be able to do that? How would you expect us to maintain a profit margin on your account?"

They had no answer for that. Saying no was powerful.

❋

A gentleman named Jim Camp wrote a book essentially talking about how powerful getting to "No" is. While the book *Getting to Yes*, from the professors at Harvard is a huge contribution to the field of negotiations, equally as important is Camp's *Start with No*.

When you push somebody to "No", it generally elicits an emotional reaction. Usually, unlike the unemotional "No" in the email that I sent, the answer "No" makes people mad.

In Camp's book, he recommends a component that encourages you to put out an offer that is so crazy; people will say no. It gets people upset, and then you build up from it. That's one of his negotiation tactics. I don't necessarily agree with that tactic. Often, I think it is only useful on rare occasions. However, I believe the power of no is hugely important, and small businesses do not use it enough. They are often afraid of losing a customer or not having the best supplier. There are so many customers and suppliers in the market that you don't have to accept a bad deal to be successful in business. In fact, doing more effective deals is key to your success.

❀

I have a client who owns a small machining shop. His company has 12 people who work for him. His dad built the company, and now he runs it. They create small parts for the aerospace defense industry. Their customers are the major players in the aerospace industry. One of those big behemoths of a company sent him a contract not long ago. It said, "This is how much volume we want to buy from you; we're only going to commit to buying 5% of that volume. Oh, and by the way, you have to be prepared to expedite 50% of it at no additional cost."

What frustrates somebody like me is that I know that that company has sent that contract to other small machine shops, and people have signed that contract. And it kills me because there is no way a small machine shop can live up to that and stay in business. And so, in comes the power of "No".

My client, essentially said no.

Guess what?

That was all it took. They sent the new contract back, took the expediting language out, and raised the order commitment. They knew it was a ludicrous ask but were going to ask regardless because they knew they had gotten it from some people.

You don't get what you don't ask for, and "no" can be hugely significant and very important in setting your relationship parameters.

## GOOD COP/BAD COP

Good-cop/ bad-cop, is a classic negotiation strategy. We see it on TV shows all the time.

We try to do it in business too because guess what?

It often works.

I was negotiating for a small client a few years ago; it was a real estate deal. We were negotiating with one of the largest property management firms in the United States. I was faced with this good-cop/ bad-cop duo. The bad-cop was an older gentleman, and the good-cop was an "earlier in his career" gentleman.

We'd get on the phone, and the bad-cop would scream and yell, call me names, tell me I was stupid, and so many other insults. I mean, you name it, bad-cop was saying it. There is a saying that a boiling teapot eventually runs out of steam, and in my experience, leaving a boiling teapot to eventually run out of steam is often the best tactic.

So, I just let the bad-cop go. He was giving me all emotion, but not giving me any content or anything to which I can react. I sit, listen, kind of nod my head, and say, "Okay, so what I hear you saying is that you're not happy about the situation." Then I say, "So, what is it that you would like to see changed about this situation?"

After "bad-cop" takes his time going off, eventually, he runs out of steam. And then the good-cop comes in.

That's when he changes his tune, as if the solution is beyond his ability to figure out.

We hang up the call, and then, invariably, the good-cop calls me back, "I'm so sorry, Christine. I know Stephen can be tough to deal with sometimes, and I want you to know that we'll figure this out."

That conversation happened the first and the second time, so that the third time, I thought to myself, *"I'm just not in the mood for this good-cop/ bad-cop thing."*

I called the good-cop, and I said, "I have a random question for you."

"What?", he answered, knocked off-guard by my tac.

"Is it 10 minutes or 30 minutes?" I questioned him.

"What do you mean?", he asks, trying to determine what I'm getting at.

"Do you practice the good-cop/ bad-cop routine for 10 minutes or 30 minutes before I get on the phone? I just want to make sure what I need to adjust so that I'm doing something on my end accordingly." I never talked to the bad-cop again.

For me, good-cop/ bad-cop is not an efficient tool for a skilled negotiator. It's so ridiculously transparent that there's no added value in doing it. However, some think that when you are more seasoned in your negotiations, working with somebody who's not as experienced, the good-cop/ bad-cop routine can be beneficial. It raises pain, and people want to avoid pain, so they'll agree to things to get the bad-cop off their case. But, the bad-cop is, in actuality, an amazing actor. I disagree.

For me as a negotiator, I just don't need to deal with the acting. Can we just like get to the real stuff and put this other stuff aside? Because it's not very helpful.

I prefer a no-nonsense approach to negotiations.

And, once you practice the skills in this book, you will too.

## GRATITUDE

Gratitude is such a fascinating topic when it comes to negotiation. Especially right now, because every day, there are more and more gratitude books. I see new podcasts on gratitude and people talking about the need to have gratitude from the stage. People are selling programs around helping you develop more gratitude, which I think is fantastic, up to a certain point.

Just like many other things that are great until they start to get abused. In negotiation, what I've seen a lot is how, especially for women and people of color, that the subject of gratitude can be sometimes morphed into a tool almost for abuse or keeping people down.

It's kind of like, "Well, you should just be grateful for the scraps I've thrown to you and just live with it." It becomes part of the voice in our heads that we are negotiating with, and we have to shut that voice down.

It goes back to what we talked about earlier in the book. It is essential to be very conscientious of that voice when you are in a negotiation. Benefactors and Ambassadors are good in this area. They will use gratitude as a tool because they tend to be focused more on relationships.

Mavericks and Champions can start to use it a little bit as a weapon, and you've got to be very careful with that. If you are somebody who expresses a lot of gratitude, that's great, but do not allow that to dissuade you from asking for more of what you want.

When you are at the table, people will sometimes question your gratitude. I've had situations in negotiations where it feels like some guy is coming over and figuratively patting me on the head. As though to say, "Christine, there, there, I know you just don't quite get it.", or, "You know what, this is what you should be happy with, and you should just kind of take this and accept it. It is the best that we can do."

I hate that because it's often not the best that they can do. When somebody starts to use that language or tries to treat you in this condescending and obsequious manner, be very careful with that. When somebody's starting to use gratitude as a weapon to get you to agree to something, take a step back. Walk far away from that table and take stock of what they're saying and what they are asking you to do.

When people espouse the concept of gratitude in this way, they're using it in a very patronizing manner. When I'm talking about gratitude being used or manipulated in negotiation, I'm actually talking about shaming somebody or having that person settle for less than they want. It comes from a shame-place; you *should* be grateful. So, it's from the position of "should-ing", which may be different from being grateful for the life you have or shifting your energy from negative toxic victim to what's working.

It is that aspect where somebody is using gratitude to make you feel shameful because you shouldn't want more, you shouldn't expect more, and you shouldn't be asking me for more. That "should" piece is significant. It is all about: "you shouldn't do that; you should be happy with what I'm giving you." I see this a lot with people in job negotiations. Or, dealing with these big Goliath organizations, many small businesses and entrepreneurs are told: "you should be grateful that this is what I'm giving you. I'm a big client. I am a marquee account. You should be willing to take a hit on your profitability because my name and my logo matter." Sometimes it does, and sometimes it doesn't. You need to know when it doesn't. Be prepared, know your numbers, and do a proper analysis.

When prepared, if somebody tries to use gratitude as a weapon, it's tough for them to play that game with you. Because you know what it is and what it's not. You can combat that by having that knowledge.

There are different types of bullies in the world, right? There are the bullies who bully you because they're aggressive. And then there are the bullies who bully because they're passive-aggressive. Know which one you're dealing with and always be willing to walk away

## AGREEMENT ON THE PROCESS

The big thing to talk about when you're getting agreement on the processes is how to communicate. We're going to communicate via email or via text. We're going to have weekly meetings, and they're going to be this long. This is who's going to be in attendance, and this is who's going to take notes. We're going to send out the notes and allow you to agree or disagree with them and make corrections and changes. This is who's going to be involved once we get close to having a deal. This is who needs to sign off on it from an approvals perspective. This is how long we expect those approvals to take.

Knowing the process and making sure this process is transparent is incredibly powerful in driving and maintaining leverage, especially as a smaller company. Try to keep control of taking incredible notes at your meeting. If you can, have a second person, whose only job is to write notes.

If you're the business owner and don't have a team of people, try to find somebody to capture everything that gets said. That way, you can summarize the notes and send them to the more prominent organization. One, it shows leadership and incentive. Two, it puts you in the driver's seat of how that communication is going to transpire. Then they get to look at them and review them. They have three days to send you comments and corrections back, and if they don't send comments and corrections, your notes are correct. If you set that rule upfront, it is harder for them to come back and renegotiate stuff that has been agreed to unless there's a really good reason to do that.

## TOOLS

A few quick thoughts on tools. For note taking, I am a huge fan of the Rocketbook (www.rocketbook.com). This tool allows you to write handwritten notes and upload them to the cloud with easy organization. The app transcribes your notes and they are automatically saved to whatever file you designate. I am also a fan of Evernote because I can throw anything into it, do a search, and find something in seconds based on how I tag things. It is fully integrated with Rocketbook too, as an added bonus. When I save files, I always put YEAR MONTH DAY TIME_File Name. For some, this may be a bit old-fashioned. but it allows me to manage my files easily. Even though I am American, I use a 24-hour time stamp. I use this for managing versions. Personally, I find it better than using any version control in other tools.

# 5

# ON THE ELEMENTS OF ATTITUDE

*Ask for more of what you want.*

Attitude is essential. It goes back to one of the things that we talked about earlier in the book around knowing you can be you—having that sense of how not to negotiate against yourself. Your attitude drives whether or not you're going to achieve the results you want to achieve. And again, to some people, this may sound a little woo-woo. I'm always going to put it out there because that's just kind of who I am. Things like how you get on the phone, how you present yourself, and how you present yourself on Zoom are essential, as most of us are doing virtual negotiations. I haven't done a face-to-face negotiation in almost 20 years. My negotiations have not had to be in person. Most of the large companies I've negotiated with, as counterparts, have distributed negotiation teams that sit in various countries across the globe, and sometimes even they have not met. The need to physically be in the presence of somebody to negotiate has not been very often for me.

. . .

Having an attitude that is conveyed across the phone or over Zoom is essential. And this is the *woo-woo* part, are you ready? Smile when you talk. It makes such a big difference. You can hear the smile, and it automatically lifts your attitude; it automatically gives you more confidence.

Some people have said to me, "Oh, Christine, I feel like that puts me in a weak position." I disagree with that. The thing is, they might have a smile on their face, but they're not really smiling. So, you really need to smile from the inside out. Automatically, by doing that, you create the opportunity for being open. Because you are more open to hearing what somebody has to say, you invite people to want to help you solve a problem. Thus, as woo-woo as that might sound to some people, it's accurate. I've had seasoned negotiators; CEOs, CFOs, and board of directors' level people comment that because I'm smiling, "It makes it so much nicer to work with you." Exactly.

That is one of the big things you can do to help boost your attitude. I also meditate and have mantras that I say. Sometimes, when going into a tough negotiation, I may have some difficulties with my counterpart. If something about my counterpart's style or personality doesn't make me feel good, I will sit down. Sometimes it's in my car, sometimes it's in the bathroom, on my sofa, or at my desk; I'll close my eyes. I'll say, "I am confident. I believe in myself. And I deserve this, whatever this is." And I will just say this over and over and over. And there have been times when I'll be in my car, saying this to myself. And I get animated, and I yell it. I believe in myself, I am confident; people will walk by, and I get these weird looks. That's okay because I'm controlling the one person, the only person I can manage in the negotiation. That is me. I have 100% control over my attitude in the negotiation.

.   .   .

J eb Blount wrote a book called *Inked* that was published early in 2020. He talks about the importance of controlling your emotions. You have control over all of those things. That attitude aspect is critical for you to get more out of your negotiation.

I t's much harder to pretend you're angry or be angry at somebody who's smiling at you. Now, it's doable. I mean, somebody smiling and being happy about what they are doing can infuriate somebody in the opposite mental state. They want you to feel in a negative mental state. However, I choose whether to move into a negative mental state or not.

One year, my husband and I were traveling. We were supposed to be traveling with our daughters to Montana. And this was when it was my first year at Harvard Business School.

The plan was that we would be leaving on Christmas Eve. As we were preparing for our journey, we heard on the radio that there was this thing called a "blue flu". Disgruntled pilots were calling in sick with the flu, even though they weren't sick. This was when Northwest still existed as an airline. That tells you how long ago it was.

Our flight was scheduled for the next morning at 5:30 AM. Our phone rang around two in the morning, and they told us they had to cancel our flights. They booked us on a flight on Christmas Day. Our kids were in the 3rd, 4th, and 5th grades at the time, so we did not want to travel on Christmas Day. The kids still believed in Santa, and how would we explain to them what Santa would do? How does he get to us if we're not where we're supposed to be?

Christmas day comes, and we get to the airport. And guess what? The pilots called in sick again, only this time Northwest had not called us to tell us that they had to cancel our flight. Next to me, at check-in, there was a gentleman who was practically leaning across the counter. He was screaming at the poor person behind the counter, who had a massive line of miserable customers. This guy was just furious, and everybody in the area heard him.

I approached the counter. The person helping me is just looking at this guy; everybody is looking at this guy. I looked at the person helping me and said, "First, I just want to thank you for being here on Christmas Day, so that I could go see my family and my kids can go see their grandparents." I said, "But, I'm really curious why you decided to work on Christmas Day."

"My wife died four years ago," he responded, "and I have no reason to celebrate Christmas anymore."

I kept thinking, *'What if that guy, who was screaming and yelling across the desk, were speaking that way to the person helping me? A man who was working there because he had lost his wife.'*

I didn't know that man's story. I asked him a question, he answered with his story, and we had a fantastic conversation as a result. The next thing I knew, he had booked my entire family in first class on a different airline at their cost, just because I was nice to him.

So, who do you think had the better experience in that situation? It certainly wasn't the guy screaming at the person trying to help him. It was the first time my kids got to fly first class, and it was such a highlight.

It's such a fantastic story in our family's history because it was an excellent lesson for me and an opportunity to teach our daughters. The power of being kind and generous should not elicit that kind of payback because you should be nice and kind in any situation, in my opinion. Kindness can elicit a boomerang of kindness, though you shouldn't expect it.

I have stories like that all over the place, how just being nice and having that in a negotiation, having that smile on my face, and the appreciation of being honored meeting a new person and being able to help find ways to create opportunities for everybody in the negotiation. That's an honor. It's a fantastic thing to be able to have those kinds of human interactions.

When you approach negotiation with an expectation that this is an honor to interact with other people in this way, it completely transforms how the negotiation takes place.

## DEALING WITH DIFFICULT PEOPLE

There are people who are more on the narcissistic spectrum, where there's something that's driving them not to think of anything other than themselves.

People who don't want to find ways to cooperate nicely with others, but that's incredibly rare. I have met a couple of them, and they are doozies of stories, but they are infrequent. In my 30 years of negotiating, I can count those people on one hand, and they don't even fill up the hand, so there are three of them. With most people, you can move them out of that kind of aggressive state.

The first thing is making sure to ask questions in the right way. This is true whether somebody is in an angry condition or not in a negotiation. When I say negotiation, I want to take a moment to say that I'm not just talking about negotiation, like in a business. You might be a parent, and your teenager, wants to borrow the car. Well, let me tell you that he or she is approaching that as a negotiation, and you probably should too.

We're negotiating all the time. In every single relationship we have, whether it's with a child, a parent, a boss, an employee, a supplier, a customer, or an investor, we are negotiating all the time. When I say negotiation, I want to make sure that everyone understands that it's an all-encompassing concept that applies to every one of your relationships.

Disarming the Champion is done by how you ask questions.

As I said, it's not just disarming the Champion; this is true across everything. The first thing to do is to avoid 'why' questions.

I have a mentor named Blair Dunkley. Blair is a fantastic guy, super smart, and heart-driven. He has this whole methodology around mind models. It is something that I have always done, but he helped me put this framework around it. It's about not asking 'why' questions of other people. When you ask somebody why it immediately puts the person who hears it on the defensive, it is accusatory. Asking - why did you not do it this way?, implies that you think that there's a better way of doing it and that the person you're asking the question should have done it that in a better way, even though they don't know what that better way might have been.

Any form of "why" question implies the same sentiment - Why haven't you? Why should you? Why could you? Why won't you?

Those are all very accusatory statements, and they put people in a defensive position. If you're trying to build cooperation, and if you're trying to add on those successive small wins, avoid using the question 'why?'. Instead, focus on 'what?', and 'how?' questions.

Another word that opens the door is - might. Instead of saying should, could, and would, use might.

If you say - 'What might you do?', 'What might you do in this situation?', it opens up possibilities for the person whom you've asked the question. It permits them to think beyond something that they are doing right now or that you feel that they should be doing or could be doing. It allows them to explore options. One of the big things that I have seen in all of my negotiations is that it's rare for people to let their counterparts to explore.

## WHAT, HOW AND MIGHT

We had a problem. We tried something, and it didn't work. We tried something else, and that didn't work. We tried something else, and even that didn't work. The fourth thing we tried, guess what? It worked. Now, for every problem, we use that fourth thing, even though it isn't necessarily the right thing.

But, we get stuck when we think about things in that way. We keep using that as a solution for every problem that has any similarity to the original problem. Though there could be many other alternatives that would yield far better outcomes. As part of our attitude, asking questions around how you might do something is significant, which has a significant impact on allowing everyone to participate in the negotiation to think about possibilities.

The first time I talked about the notion of possibilities in negotiation as a valuable concept, I laughed at myself, and thought about how my attorney friends would laugh at that notion. Any negotiation we enter into, we assume that there's value for all the parties involved in the talks as we advance. That value may not exist today, but we're entering into an agreement based on the hope of the benefit happening in the future. Suppose we don't permit ourselves to think about what's possible. In that case, we lose the ability to hope for a long-term solution that is mutually beneficial for everyone involved.

When we allow ourselves to be open, using 'what' and 'how' and asking using 'might,' it also lets us open our minds about how we think about things. In a Chapter 6, we are going to cover the topic of intentional listening. Before we get to the listening stage, we begin by asking 'what' and 'how' questions and using the word 'might'. This creates opportunities for our counterparts to think in terms of possibilities.

Remember, we are at the proverbial negotiation table. When I am at that table with my counterpart, I am not the most important person. When I am in direct dialogue with my counterpart, my role is to learn as much information as possible. That way, I can refine my hypotheses about what the counterpart can and cannot do. Using 'what' and 'how' questions, and asking what might be possible, gives me more information. That helps me refine what is possible, what's doable because I know my side of the equation.

## WIN-WIN

*Stop trying to win your negotiations.*

I've used 'win' several times in this book already because it is something that in negotiation, people talk about all the time, and we do win things. Yet, I'm not too fond of the win-win concept, because people don't necessarily use it the way they should. I also do not like the idea of winning in a negotiation because it turns the negotiation into a competition. We're not playing soccer.

Some people think we are. The Champion thinks we are playing a sport, and somebody has to win, and somebody has to lose. The Ambassador, which I am, does not like that mentality. Champions deal from a place of scarcity; there's one thing and I either get it, or they get it. That means, one of us is going to win it, and one is going to lose it.

For Ambassadors, negotiating from a position of abundance, there's more than enough of whatever it is to share across the larger population of people who want it. So, being calm becomes essential when you start to feel emotion getting involved.

With emotions like anger, anxiousness, nervousness, sadness emerge, consider taking a break. Be introspective. Ask yourself what about the situation is bothering you specifically. Sit with it for a while and put words to the emotion and reason for it.

In many situations, I will be completely transparent about how I feel. I am calm in stating it but there is power in acknowledging how something is impacting me in the negotiation. Not only that, I have no problem asking my counterparts how they feel about a situation or a solution. Suppose I'm negotiating with somebody who's a Benefactor, they are more feeling-oriented in their decision making. In that case, that's a huge component of how they're going to evaluate that deal. They're going to want to know that it feels right for them. If they are a modern communicator, that intuition aspect is crucial. I want to test that to make sure that it is true or not.

## DIFFERENT STYLES

Everyone has a different trigger point to emotional issues. I become a Champion when I see an absolute injustice, and I will come to the defense of the person or organization for whom I know that injustice is taking place. But, I do it in a very different way than you may, depending on your style.

When I am in my Champion style, I get super calm. I drop my voice, it goes into a monotone; it is very pragmatic. I employ 100% facts; cold and calculating. You do not want to be negotiating with me when I am in that state. My full-on Champion is scary. I am calm, in total control of my emotions, and I'm clear; it is a striking sight to behold, not comfortable for the person on the other side. I don't mean it to be. I am trying to elicit an extreme reaction from that person. However, that calmness is different from a Champion who throws a tantrum and starts yelling and calling somebody names. It's still a Champion mentality in the negotiation; it's just that we're expressing it in totally different ways. My calm demeanor as a Champion will yield better results than somebody angry and expressing that anger.

. . .

O ne of the things that I love most about negotiation is that it gives me the ability to be creative. The best solutions are innovative solutions. Because again, as an Ambassador, for me, it's about finding these disparate things, these things that are disconnected, or appear disconnected, from one another. I like to look at the sides objectively and figure out - Wait, is that actually disconnected? I'll take that idea and say, "Okay, at what point does that idea, and this thing relate?" And I'm doing this in my head; it's not like I'm drawing a diagram or anything. Can I make it relate? Are there aspects or attributes of it that are similar, or tangential, or parallel?

I used to be a career advisor at Harvard Business School for many years. One of my students was challenging. Harvard prides itself on having a large percentage of its students having jobs before they graduate. This student was just struggling. He was from France. He had worked at an oil and gas company. He was a petrochemical engineer, but, he wanted to move into the pharmaceutical industry. Talk about a difference. Now, when I say he worked in oil and gas, I mean that he worked on oil rigs out in the middle of the sea. This appeared to have nothing in common with working in the pharmaceutical industry.

One day, I said, "Of course, it has everything to do with the oil and gas industry. There's a complete correlation there. Most pharmaceuticals use petrochemicals in the development of pills and tablets, and all sorts of things. So, now we have a common theme; we know there is a relationship between petrochemicals and pharmaceuticals. How do we explain it and rewrite your resume, and recreate your messaging in a way that positions you with a pharmaceutical company? Although you have zero experience, and nothing that you've done appears to have a relationship."

We were successful in getting him a position with one of the top pharmaceutical companies in Europe.

## BRINGING CREATIVITY TO THE TABLE

*Define your ask in a way that makes it valuable to your counterpart.*

Creativity comes to the negotiation table all the time, in terms of how you bring in information, communications from the past, where somebody says they're willing to do something, only to go back on their word later.

One example of how I brought creativity to the table was when I was negotiating with a software giant (Goliath). It was quite a few years ago, after Enron and all of the garbage that had gone on with funky accounting was exposed. When the dot-com bubble burst, one of the reasons it was bursting is because they were doing funny things with their money. They'd sell something, they would get paid for it upfront, and they would count it all as revenue. But, they still had to earn it over time, which is why the government changed the accounting rules. You couldn't recognize revenue until you earned it. If you have a 12-month software licensing fee, you can only recognize revenue every month instead of all upfront at once. That situation drove revenue recognition, rules, and legislation. Revenue recognition is now a massive thing in accounting.

I'm sitting there talking with this software giant, which is a publicly traded company. The salesperson sits in the room, and we're asking for something. It was prevalent at the time for salespeople and tech companies to say this, "We can't do that. It's a revenue recognition problem."

I went to their annual report, published with the SEC, and looked. Included in their annual report had to be a description of what their revenue recognition policy was. At my next meeting, I took a copy of the company's annual report. I handed it to the salesperson and said, "Here is your revenue recognition policy. Please explain to me how this policy impacts this request." Many people would not do that. That was a very creative way of taking something that the salesperson was telling me was a not possible thing. I diffused it by saying, "your company communication says that this doesn't fall into that issue. You can do it, so explain how it fits." I wasn't calling him a liar. I was challenging him to tell me how what we've proposed does not fit into this policy.

Few people would have gone and researched to understand that a portion of it comes down to being creative with what you're doing yourself. I had a client who used software once that they just didn't know how to use. There had to be a different way of evaluating how they used the software. How to determine what they used it for, and who used it. Knowing that and finding those pieces of information made it possible to save millions of dollars for that client.

I had a client who went through a divestiture; their company was splitting into three separate companies. They wanted to take a software contract and apply it to each of the three new entities. The software vendor said they couldn't do that. So, I researched and looked at all of the contract relationships, which was almost a 30-year history of contracts. I went through and audited, looking for precise language to find that they were able to do what we were asking for just two years ago. We could now look at what changed. What was it that made them stop being able to do this? Can we take that clause and bring it back again? Because I found that clause, we were able to resurrect it. We were able to save millions and millions of dollars for the client, just with a little bit of creative research.

## A POWERFUL ATTITUDE

The biggest thing in attitude is putting a smile on your face. It makes a huge difference. Making sure that, even if you're not feeling powerful, that you do things to help yourself feel strong. Whether it's a mantra, a stance, or something else.

One of my daughters is a professional nanny. She had a dispute with one of the families for which she was caring for their children. The mother and father owed her money. They were not going to pay her. They considered that because she was young and good-natured, they could get away with not paying her for her work.

She was very nervous about the conversation; she felt very much like she didn't have power in the situation. The mom was a very aggressive person. I told my daughter, "Do not sit down. When you are talking to them, stand up and keep both feet planted on the ground, it will help center you." I continued, "If you still feel vulnerable, stand behind the kitchen island, stand behind something solid that you can hold on to, something to help you feel rooted. That can help give you strength, it's artificial strength, but it's still strength. It still does something to our psyche."

There are things you can do physically to help boost your attitude. It can be doing a workout before you have a big negotiation meeting. Maybe repeating a declaration, or putting a smile on your face. Having that right attitude, that frame of mind that you're going to solve a problem and find a solution that will work for both parties, is enormous. And be positive in how you're communicating with yourself. Make sure that you're just repeating good things to put yourself in a good mood.

We've gone over quite a bit in this chapter on the power of your attitude. Your attitude determines whether you will successfully achieve the things you want to get out of your negotiation. Your ability to believe in what you are asking for will drive whether somebody desires to give it to you. Your ability to ask in an uplifting and positive way will prompt how somebody interacts with you, and determines whether or not they want to give it to you. People just genuinely like working with more affable individuals who are easier to work with.

When you feel uplifted, powerful, capable, and your attitude is positive, it translates into your negotiation. It translates into the strength of words that you use; it translates into your posture, and translates into everything about your being. When you're in that state, your counterpart reacts to it, and they typically react positively to it. In the next chapter, we're going to be talking about another colossal negotiation component; the power of intentional listening.

# 6

# ON THE POWER OF INTENTIONAL LISTENING

*Listening is a full contact sport.*

Intentional listening is what I consider to be a full-contact sport. It requires all of you, all of your being, all of your senses to listen with intent.

People will talk about active listening. The challenge I have with the concept of active listening, is it doesn't involve all of the senses. It's more around waiting to speak until somebody finishes speaking. But, active listening doesn't include how important it is to observe all of the aspects of how someone is communicating to you. It's more what you do with your ears and not about overall communication.

Intentional listening is something that you do by paying attention to somebody's words, tone, and non-verbals as well as observing the cues they give you about who they are. When you observe how somebody is behaving, their body language, their nonverbal cues, and micro-expressions, you can see those nanosecond moments when somebody does something telling. It reflects more on their face than it does in the words that they are speaking.

A UCLA study suggests that 93% of communication has nothing to do with the words coming out of somebody's mouth. It has to do with tone and body language.

I've traveled outside of the United States and negotiated with people whose primary language is not English. When they speak their native language, I can tell by their body language whether they're happy or frustrated. Even if I don't fully understand their language, I can tell whether they have contempt for what's said. If I see some other major emotions, I can tap into them because I have that observation intentionally.

The intentional listening activity is a very comprehensive activity, to pay attention to what's not spoken, but rather, what's being communicated overall in the discussion.

As Americans, we tend to speak very, very quickly. Again, I'm intentional about my communication, and I make sure to speak slowly. I will ask people to please let me know if I'm talking too quickly. In a post-pandemic world, wearing a mask is challenging for people who have hearing loss and who read lips. I started using a pad of paper, especially in video meetings. Using a pad of paper or a small erasable whiteboard to make notes or draw pictures is a useful tool to help overcome those challenges. But even still, much communication happens with people's eyes. You may not hear the words that are being said and need to ask somebody to repeat them. But, you can tell by how they're communicating with their eyes, what their general disposition is, on what it is that you're saying.

## KNOWLEDGE IS RELATIONSHIP POWER

Knowledge is power, and I love to learn. I love it when I'm wrong about something. When I make a statement, and somebody says that I'm completely wrong, I don't get upset about that. I'm like, "Oh, really, what's it supposed to be?"

When they tell me, I'll go kind of down a little bit of a rabbit hole to verify it. I'll add context to what I just learned so that I have a deeper level of knowledge. It's incredible to me that one of the benefits of being a lifelong learner is that it allows me to build relationships with people on multiple levels.

A question people have asked me many times, "What are some of the things that I should learn and understand to be able to connect with people?"

My number one thing is to learn about pets, study the different breeds of dogs and cats. Because many, many people have them, and animal lovers love to talk about their pets. I never ask about a photo of a child or anything like that because I know too many women (or their partners) who have not been able to conceive, or women who have just had miscarriages. That question can be kind of hurtful for them. It's unintentional on the part of the person making the query, but it can create an awkward situation. You never know what someone's personal situation is, so unless they voluntarily bring up their kids, don't ask.

When it comes to dogs and cats, I can sit and talk about Russian blue cats and speak about borzois and Italian grey-hounds. I can see somebody's dog picture, and immediately recognize it. That typically opens the conversation; that's an Irish Wolfhound, a fascinating breed. It's got hunting characteristics. How is it with children?

I can get into detail about them, and people love that. It's such an easy icebreaker. I have many books about dog breeds.

My husband even tries to stump me on my canine knowledge. Recently, he sent me a picture, with the message - "I bet you can't guess this one." I responded that it's a giant Commodore; they look like big mops. He doesn't try to test my canine trivia anymore.

I will say the love of pets and the pet industry is very much of a Western culture thing. It is expanding throughout the globe, and people in other cultures are starting to embrace the importance of having pets and what pets can mean in somebody's life.

I also studied wine a lot. I know a lot about wine, which is helpful in some of the higher touch points negotiating circles.

I also study history, architecture, and agriculture. These are topics that I keep in my arsenal of ice-breakers, ready to use with all sorts of people.

Earlier in the book, I told you about the car story, well, the dealership manager was a dog-sled racer. I could sit and talk about the Iditarod. I could speak about standard poodles and the controversy of them racing in the Iditarod. It is some random topic about which I have a little bit of knowledge. I have retained it, which I can then pull out later to build a relationship with somebody.

## ICEBREAKERS

Icebreakers are essential. I didn't talk much about icebreakers in the earlier chapter about initiating the conversation because, ironically, icebreakers are more about intentional listening than they are about initiating a conversation.

Icebreakers can be incredibly useful when you research the person you're going to be working with, your counterpart. It helps you understand some of the things they love to do, their hobbies, and their interests. People often have their Facebook profiles on private, so sometimes you can't see them. You can see it on LinkedIn, where profiles usually are not confidential because people want you to find them on LinkedIn. You can do a Google search to see what you can find on your counterpart, but that's only effective if they are an individual operator. If they work within a large corporate structure, it may be very hard to find anything about their private life online.

It can be beneficial to see where you have some commonalities, have similar interests, or have very different passions.

I'm a motorcyclist, and people tend to think, "Oh, my gosh, a woman who rides a motorcycle, that's kind of an unusual thing."

If you see my hair, then you know I have crazy hair; I dye it all sorts of different colors, all the time. I've been doing it this way for 20 years. For some people, it creates an issue. They get very offended that I would do that. Though, for the most part, the reaction I hear is; "Oh, my gosh, that's so cool that you do that. I love your hair."

If somebody sees my photo and reads my LinkedIn profile, they're going to get a particular view of who I am. I'm very direct in my LinkedIn profile; I share some of my story upfront. I talk about being an unwed mom and being homeless and going to Harvard. That communicates something about me to a counterpart, to the very few, if any, who have viewed my profile.

If I am entering into a negotiation with you - I guarantee you; I have looked you up. I've researched you on Google. I've looked at your LinkedIn profile. If I can, I will have looked at your Facebook profile and your Instagram. I look so that I can get a sense of who you are. Because, by having a sense of who you are, it helps me truncate and shorten that relationship development process because I know what's important to you.

If you love cooking, that's great. I love cooking, too.

Suppose you enjoy doing something that I don't enjoy, like four-wheeling. In that case, I'm going to ask you a question because my husband does want to do four-wheeling. He's all excited about the new Ford Bronco and wants to go off-roading. That's something for me to ask about and learn about because I love to learn. I can then retain that information, via my CRM, for the next person that I meet who has that same interest. And, the knowledge shared with me by my counterpart will help me build that next relationship.

S hould you let your counterpart know you have researched them?

The answer about whether you've done research or not, is

dependent on who you are and who your counterpart is. There have been times when I have said, "I've done my homework." I want to put the person I'm dealing with on notice that I'm not a pushover. I am somebody they need to take seriously.

If I'm negotiating with a Champion, I'm more likely to comment that I've done my homework, partly because I know they won't have done theirs. It puts us in a bit of a power struggle in terms of how that relationship will unfold. Still, I want them to know that I know something about them and take the conversation seriously.

Then there are other times. For somebody that is more of a peer, I would find more natural ways of finding out about you and having you disclose that through questions. I would weave in non-confrontational questions;

Do you have a sense of what it is that we might be including in a meeting?

What are you up to tonight?

Did you have a long drive in?

I would look to create opportunities for you to have a conversation with me to disclose what you are comfortable sharing with me.

Most people don't assume that I've researched them. Because of that, I want to make sure that they have the opportunity to disclose to me what they want to, and then I build on that.

## GETTING TOO PERSONAL

The notion of getting too personal is fascinating because this plays heavily into family negotiation and partnerships with friends and family.

When you're doing business together with somebody with whom you have a very close relationship, there comes the point where we have to disconnect, because negotiation is inherently emotional. When we have a tight relationship with a person that we're entering into a business arrangement with, that we can sometimes lose sight of ourselves in that relationship. We get all excited about the possibilities, and we focus on how amazing it's going to be.

We don't think about the things that could go wrong; we don't plan well enough for the risk. Many times, when you see many partnerships like this unfold, friendships, family relationships are destroyed.

People get stuck into certain behaviors or a cycle of how they work together. One party may not be as forthcoming when things are not working for them. They may not be as forceful in terms of defining what it is that they want out of the negotiation. There becomes this part of the relationship where one person may feel taken advantage of, and the other person is the one taking the advantage. It can create a good deal of animosity. If you're not conscientious about it, it will impact your business and your relationships very negatively.

## WHEN NEGOTIATIONS GET PERSONAL

When we're talking about negotiation, and I've said this earlier, negotiation is in everything we do.

If you think that you don't need to be a good negotiator, just ask anybody who's going through a divorce. The reality is that if you can figure out how to negotiate effectively, especially if you have a child, it's generally to that child's benefit that you guys figure out how to work together. It is essential to negotiate with a clear view of what you want and why you want it and know how it will impact the counterpart, especially in a divorce situation.

I have a client whom I'm advising in a divorce negotiation. She didn't want to work with an attorney, neither does her soon-to-be-ex-husband. They've been legally separated for many years, but, are now finalizing a divorce. They're selling a big piece of property. She's asked me to negotiate on her behalf with her soon-to-be-ex, to deal with the escrow as it comes out, once they sell the property. Once they sell this enormous piece of property, they have to distribute funds out of escrow.

The thing is, she was not in a position to negotiate. Every time they communicated, it caused her massive amounts of anxiety and stress. She had her money locked up and tied up in this property for years because her ex didn't want to sell it. He had a lot of money, as he had gotten an enormous inheritance. He had the power; at least, she felt that he had control. She'd been living on virtually nothing, and he had millions of dollars. At the same time, all of her money was wrapped up into this piece of property.

He came into the negotiation demanding that she pay for investments he made on the property, even though she didn't agree to the investments or permit him to do that. My client knew that she was not in a position to negotiate with him because she would get so exasperated by the discussion that she would always give up. Unfortunately, that would have cost her hundreds of thousands of dollars. Luckily, by having me negotiate on her behalf, I was able to keep the emotions out of the negotiation and to come up with a fair and equitable settlement.

I work with a non-profit organization called She Is Hope LA. We work with newly minted single moms, many of whom have zero credit because their husbands handled the finances and had all the credit cards. So, they've gotten the kids and nothing else. We help provide them with education on how to get jobs and the resources to rebuild their lives. The unequal distribution of power happens often in marriages, very often leaving women, and some men, feeling they lack strength at the negotiation table.

This negotiation concept is 100% applicable in your world, whether you're going through a divorce, buying a house or car, anything that you're negotiating in your personal life. As it is in a business situation, whether you're working with customers, buying products or services, getting investors, or selling your business. This notion of relationship and having conflict in a partnership situation where you're with family or a close friend can be a very challenging issue.

Suppose the parties involved don't feel that they have the same or equal right to voice their problems and concerns, and there is no process set up for that to happen. In that case, I encourage partnerships with families and close friends to meet regularly with an unrelated third party. Not a lawyer, probably a business coach or an executive coach. The third party can be a sounding board to address issues. I think that it helps to resolve problems before they start to fester and cause damage.

## MARRIAGE AS A NEGOTIATION

It's very challenging to approach marriage as a negotiation for many people. It's challenging to broach the topic of a prenup or some legally contractual aspect of the relationship. The reality is, if you're getting married, once you sign that marriage certificate, your marriage license is a legal contract that goes with that relationship.

My husband and I have joked over time, and this may be controversial when I say it, that couples should have a renewable five-year contract.

There should be a contract to enter into it, and then you have to renegotiate it every five years. Then you can decide to enter into a new one or not, and you would have already included your breakup terms in it. There will be people appalled by that conversation. I'm sure some people will quit this book right now, or I will get a lot of nasty social media comments. But the genesis of that conversation was really - How to create opportunities to minimize damage caused by divorce? Especially when roughly 50% of marriages end in divorce.

We don't work this way; we don't have a contract, but we think it's an intriguing concept. That if you approach a relationship, either figuratively or literally, having a contract that you agree that you're going to sit down and re-explore what is working, what's not working, and how to move forward.

Do you want to move forward?

How do you move forward?

It's a real conversation. The idea of our discussion around it was really about how you put some structure around it and encourage that kind of talk.

Without having that conversation, you're likely not going to have a long-lasting marriage. I know I'm fortunate. We know many people in our circle who have been happily married for 20 plus years. It's always interesting for me when I listen to them and think about our relationship. We have these conversations all the time, conversations in which we talk about what is and isn't working.

My husband and I, not long ago, did something unique. I was on a call and I said something, which to me, was completely innocuous. I was networking with somebody I had met at an event that we were both on, a virtual networking thing. We had this call, and he asked me where I live. So, I told him where I live. My husband overheard me, and I could instantly see that he was furious. He got so upset with me that he shushed me while I was on the phone, which did not sit well with me.

I got off the phone, and was not happy. And, my husband was not pleased with me either. It mortified me that he did that while I was on the phone, and this was with a senior person I was speaking with, somebody I could partner with in the future. My husband came to me and said, "I know I didn't handle that right. But, you scare me when you trust somebody that much. It's not safe for you to do that."

I said, "You're right; it's not safe. I don't mean to scare you, but I did not like how you handled that."

It was the first time in our 27 years of marriage, almost 30 years of being together, that he had expressed that fear.

His reaction was new, so, that's a new term in our contract. I don't tell people where I live anymore. And that is that. That's a kind of an example of a clause in the contract changing.

The happiest couples I know, who have been married for a long time, have those kinds of discussions and openness to talk about what isn't working. Whatever part of your life, whether it's your financial life, your sexual life, your kids, whatever it is, that transparency and open conversation are of the utmost importance. You need those clear conversations because marriage is the ultimate negotiation.

## FORMAL AND INFORMAL CONTRACTS

We're going to discuss contracts in more detail in Part III of the book, but as they relate to intentional listening, it's worth giving an overview here.

Contracts can be formal or informal. Written or verbal. Sealed with a signature or with a handshake.

My contract with my husband is formal in that it is a legally binding relationship; recognized by law and government. But, a lot of the aspects of how we approach our contract are informal. Having that recognition and knowing that a contract doesn't have to be a legal document, is essential for clarity here. You can have it be an informal contract, but it's still a contract.

I'm certainly not a marriage counsellor or relationship counsellor. There are some topics that I think is a conversation that couples need to have with professionals. I do believe; when we're talking about the notion of intentional listening, that it behooves people to think in totality about their relationship.

I know a woman whose long-term boyfriend wanted to have a prenup before marriage. She was very offended by the concept of a prenup. It is entirely anecdotal, but my experience is that men seem to be more frequently willing to ask for a prenup. Women tend to be more rejecting of that. I have to say that as

I've gotten older, I'm personally supportive of the prenup on behalf of women.

When I talked to the gentleman in the couple about the prenup, he had very specific things that he was trying to save. He was trying to save all the work that he had done. That was his work. He wanted to protect his retirement if something happened; he's terrified of being left with nothing. If, for some unforeseen reason, the relationship was not to withstand the test of time; he wanted to ensure that he had some protection around his retirement. She works in a role that doesn't have much income, and to be honest, works under the table. There are many benefits that she has with that sort of income, but it also creates some issues for her because she doesn't have the provable income to sign a mortgage. She's terrified that a prenup would preclude her from owning the property if she could not be on that mortgage. I explained to her that a prenup can actually help her. In that situation, you can structure it so that your house owner-ship is what you protect.

You protect what makes you nervous, which is a risk aspect for you, while he gets protection on the risk aspect for him.

I think that marriage and relationships are the ultimate emotional interactions. If people think logically about the essen-tial things, a prenup can be useful in certain relationships. I don't think it's always beneficial, but I believe it can help some cases. I have seen way too many women personally left with absolutely nothing because they didn't have a prenup.

## THE TWO TABOOS

There are two significant taboos, and they go in line with listening intentionally.

One of those taboos is lying. The other is disrespect.

When I went through my divorce with my first husband, the number of lies and the disrespect he showed me was astounding.

He sued me for custody when I went to Harvard. His suit stated, "the rigorous and demanding nature of Harvard Business School makes it impossible for the defendant to provide proper maternal care." It was a money grab for him. He was thinking, "Okay, she went to Harvard Business School, so I should get something out of that. He was only trying to get the kids so that I'd have to pay him money for child support because two weeks before I finished school, he dropped the case for unknown reasons.

Lying and being disrespectful are two very different components. There's a great TED Talk from Pamela Meyer. It's one of the top TED Talks in history.

Her speech is all about lying; about how we lie or are lied to an average of 10 to 100 times a day. If you don't live with your mother, you've probably lied to her within your first 5 interactions of seeing her. You'll lie to your partner as little as 1 in 3 times, or 1 in 10 times a day.

I did a presentation at the City Club in Los Angeles a few months ago. It was all about lying. We talked for over an hour and a half about lying and its role in negotiation.

According to research from multiple institutions, people hate negotiating because they automatically assume they're getting lied to; that's a regrettable situation. For some people, a white lie is still a lie; for others, a white lie is acceptable. There is also the more material kind of lie.

A white lie would be, "Oh, I didn't read your email," or "I didn't see your email." The white lie is that you did see the email, you may not have read it, but you did know that it arrived. The dog ate the homework kind of thing.

Or, you could have a material lie. Something like I talked about earlier in the book when I was doing the SAP negotiation. "We can't do that because it violates our revenue recognition policy," when in fact, it didn't violate their revenue recognition policy. That's a lie, and the salesman knew it was a lie.

Lying, to me, is a taboo in negotiation. I do not tell white lies in negotiations, and I do not tell material lies. I am also very good at discovering if somebody is telling me a material lie. I do that through research.

I n one recent negotiation with a landlord, I was representing two tenants in the same shopping mall. The landlord kept telling me all these things about how he has properties in demand. I researched. I looked at 20 properties that they had in the region that my clients operate. I found that the particular location had the highest vacancy rate of all of their properties in that region. But, the landlord kept trying to just his claim that he had high occupancy rates in the region. That's true when you look across their portfolio. But, when you look at just that location where my clients are, that's not true.

I got on the phone with him and said, "Well, I'm curious. In our previous conversation, you talked about not being willing to renegotiate certain aspects of this relationship because you have high occupancy. That's giving you confidence in terms of the discussion you and I are having. But, I'm interested because I looked at your occupancy rates. I'd like to understand how the occupancy rate in this location is different from the rest of your sites? Because your argument around occupancy is true if I look across your whole portfolio, but it's not true if I look at this location."

It was crucial to the negotiation because what he then disclosed is that they had plans to renovate that mall. They're letting leases expire and are starting to move tenants out. That's an entirely different kind of situation than "I have great occupancy."

Having done your homework and your research puts you in a power position because you can ferret out this disinformation. This ability is useful in a negotiation when you are lied to, given misinformation, or they are skirting around things. So that knowledge and that research that you've done in the preparation phase are essential to help make sure that you're getting the best possible deal.

## OTHER CULTURES

In my experience, intentional listening is even more critical when working in different cultures and with people whose primary culture is not your own. It's important to speak more slowly; it's essential to listen with every part of your body and pay attention to how they say things looking for micro expressions.

There's a gentleman named Dr. Paul Ekman, who studied many years ago at the University of Chicago, and has trained others worldwide. The TV show, *Lie to Me,* is based on his work. His work is all about the concept of micro-expressions. There's a finite number of micro-expressions that the human face has.

Every face will contort into the same look when they have certain emotions. Studying those and learning those micro-expressions is incredibly powerful, especially things around contempt and joy, and several others. Understanding those and looking at those micro-expressions to see where you stand when working with somebody whose primary language is not your own. There are definitely cultural differences, even with the same language.

I was speaking with somebody not long ago, she is a British woman living in Argentina. We were talking about American culture relative to British culture. I said something, and she said, "that's so American of you." It's true; I tend to say things like, "it's the best thing" or "that's amazing," and Europeans are looking at me going, "Seriously? Really? No. Amazing is the birth of a child. Amazing is not what you did at work."

There are different ways that different cultures approach a negotiation. In parts of Asia, for example, a verbal agreement is binding. The United States uses formal contracts more than any other culture. We try to document everything. Whereas in different cultures, that's not their style.

When I was first learning negotiation, I was working primarily in Southeast Asia. Their contracts were very thin compared to ours in the United States. I was fascinated by everything about how the different cultures in Asia negotiated. Keep in mind that Asia is a big continent, there are many cultures within Asia. You cannot say that the Chinese negotiate the same way as the Japanese, the same way as people from India, the same way as the Philippines.

In fact, in the United States, we have different cultures in how we negotiate. How you negotiate in Boston and New York is very different than how you deal in California or Seattle. All of it is different than how you negotiate in Louisiana, which uses an entirely separate legal structure. They follow Napoleonic law, so they have a completely different legal construct than we do in the rest of the United States.

Culture plays out in many behavioral aspects of negotiation, including directness. There are certain cultures where being a Champion is part of the culture, and then they back off of it. It's imperative to understand what the different cultures are.

When I was 28, I was negotiating a significant deal in Seoul, South Korea. At the time, it was incredibly rare for women to be in positions of leadership, even more so for young women. Yet, there I was. Before agreeing to take the assignment, I requested an attaché be assigned me. Someone who was South Korean and male. I needed someone who would educate me in the cultural traditions: where to sit, how to behave at dinner, who to introduce myself to first, or should I let him introduce me. I experienced tremendous success there because the person assigned to me help me understand how to navigate the culture so I wouldn't offend anyone.

The cultural divide is one of the things that is huge for me in international negotiations. One of the books that I often use to study international negotiation is not a book on international negotiation, per se. Steven Ambrose's *Undaunted Courage* talks about the Lewis and Clark Expedition across the United States.

My dad grew up on a reservation in Montana, so that expedition has always been interesting to me. I don't want to talk about the political aspects or impacts of the Lewis and Clark Expedition. They had to negotiate with more than 25 different tribes as they moved across the country. They had varying degrees of success in doing that. To me, it is a fascinating story about the importance of multicultural negotiation. I prefer calling it multicultural versus international.

Different cultures have different approaches. When you are entering into a multicultural negotiation, you need to be aware of how those different cultures behave.

A few years ago, I was negotiating a deal for a month with Euro Telecom. They had somebody on their negotiation team in London, somebody in France, somebody in India, and somebody in the United States. Each of those cultures has a unique negotiation style. It was fascinating to see how each had their individual negotiation styles and how they were reflective of their cultural styles as negotiators.

You need to be mindful of the cultures of the people you are negotiating with and how culture differs not only from country to country but region to region.

Suppose you're coming outside of the United States into the US. In that case, you should know that if you're working with somebody from New York. You will not be able to negotiate with them the same way as if you are working with somebody from my home state of Montana. In each state, there is a very different style to the way people do business. Respect and appreciate cultural differences, but focus on the person. After all, it's the person sitting in front of you that matters most.

Culture changes by latitude and longitude.

## QUESTION EXCERCISE

One of the things that I like to do when I'm teaching is to break people up into small groups and engage in this exercise.

I'll have somebody ask a question, I call that person *The Asker*. Once the question is asked, *The Asker* is not allowed say another word for 30 seconds. Thirty seconds is not that long of a time. Yet, I can tell immediately who the good intentional listeners are and who is not a good intentional listener. Very few people are very good at listening with intent. Most people expect the other people in the group to answer the question.

Invariably, if have a group of five or six people, somebody will dive right in and answer the question, they just go straight into it. That's how most people expect things to happen. Ultimately, somebody else will wait until the last second before they start to offer any contribution to the discussion, I call that person *The Observer*.

What often happens is that *The Asker* begins to mouth the answer, because they are so anxious to say something. They will be leaning out of their chair across the table in anticipation for the end of that 30 seconds, and they cannot wait any longer.

Inevitably, *The Observer* waits until the last moment and contributes something very profound and interesting to the conversation.

When the 30 seconds is over, I point out to *The Asker*, that if they had successfully interjected and put their perspective into answering the question early, they would have missed the answer that *The Observer* was waiting until the last second to give.

*The Asker* would have influenced their listeners' perspectives and swayed their natural answers. Worse, they would have potentially missed an opportunity to learn some exciting and valuable information.

It's a simple exercise. I encourage people to practice at home with friends and family, to start to get comfortable with silence.

In negotiation, silence is a potent tool. There have been many times when I am on the phone, and I'll ask a question. The other person will start to answer it before I have even finished the question. I will say nothing, so they stop, and there is silence on both sides. I just keep quiet because I know that at some point, the person on the other end of the phone is going to start talking again. I'm going to get some of the best information when someone tries to fill in that space because they're uncomfortable with that silence.

Sometimes I'll get: "Are you still there?", I assure them that I'm still there, just listening, and then they'll start talking again.

It's not the first things that come out of somebody's mouth that matter; it's the later things. That's where you can uncover essential information.

As we learned in 2020, one of the pandemic environments' challenges was not being physically present with people when we're in meetings. If we have a face-to-face negotiation or a team negotiation, our team is in the room, and we're on the phone with our counterpart. We lose the opportunity to have that final moment. The meeting is over, but people are still talking. Those are good moments to listen to the tidbits of information that get shared. People drop vital information in those moments because now they've relaxed as the meeting is over, and they often disclose things. That can be very important and valuable to create more value for all the parties involved in the discussion.

## NOTE-TAKING

I take copious notes all the time in a negotiation. Though, I prefer to have somebody taking notes to pick up on those things so that I can focus on the non-ear things.

I also ask permission to record the call to make sure that I'm not losing something. Then I just send out a transcript at the end of the call, so we both have it. Ensure that if you are recording your negotiation, you are upfront about asking permission. In some states it is illegal to record someone without their permission. Avoid the risk and ask first.

## SIT BACK AND LISTEN

It is more powerful to sit back and to listen than it is just to jump in. Again, negotiation is inherently emotional, and we are inherently emotional beings. The one most likely to gain the most from the negotiation will be the one who controls those emotions the best.

Those who can sit and calmly express themselves.

The most powerful person in any negotiation is someone who doesn't get so anxious that they have to jump in all the time. Because, when you have to jump in to include your point of view and your perspective, you are forgetting that you are not the most important person at the table. When you are in that meeting, your role is to discover your counterpart's needs and wants.

By using the power of intentional listening, you can figure out a deal that's going to create a lifetime of value for all of the parties involved. Unless you don't care about that, and it's all about haggling over something, then jump in. But, if it's something that you are expecting to have a relationship over, it behooves you to sit back and listen. Let your counterpart share and disclose what's important to them, and you pay attention to them.

# 7

# ON DAVID AND GOLIATH
# NEGOTIATIONS

*You can't win a relationship,*
*but you can get more value out of it.*

I n Chapter 4, I introduced the concept of the David and Goliath negotiations. It deserves a deeper dive into what that looks like, as there are many misnomers in these kinds of negotiations.

David and Goliath negotiations are when a smaller company (or entrepreneur) works with larger businesses, which often have extensive checks and balances systems. Getting anything approved takes forever, and you have a dozen people that have to sign off on it.

That being the case, that length of time needed to get things moving may work in your favor or against you in negotiation.

The time required on the part of a larger company to go through the approvals process, and whether that's an advantage or a disadvantage is very dependent on the deal situation.

You may have a situation where you have to make an emergency purchase because you don't have enough software, or you're using more software than what you have.

Maybe you have equipment that fails, and you need to replace it. It is not under warranty, and you need a new contract.

Perhaps, you have to have a quick change of suppliers or add a distributor. You may need to get approvals rather quickly in that negotiation.

For a larger company, that can be a disadvantage in that scenario. They just are not nimble enough and cannot act fast enough to get that put together.

My attorney friends may not like when I say this, but that's okay. In my experience, the reality is that business is often not stopped or thwarted because you don't have a complete contract.

I've seen many purchase orders executed without a contract in place with the company. It is doable, but not ideal.

With a larger company, their purchasing department and their attorneys will be very unhappy with that as a concept. But, it happens, even in mergers and acquisitions.

When you have a divestiture environment, separating companies and contracts may need to go with the detached entity. You need permissions to do that. I've never had a deal not happen because that process didn't finalize before the deal closed. Even though those processes exist in big companies, they don't have to be preventative. They don't have to prevent something from happening. It's always good to have those things finalized - the i's dotted and the t's crossed. For that, you need to consider their longer process.


## DIVESTITURES

In Part I, we looked at the negotiation process when you initiate the conversation with a large company or another party to have that process known and agreed to upfront.

Here, we're focusing on the divestiture.

Divestiture is when you have a company that sells a business unit, a product line, or some part of its business, but the business itself stays intact.

I'll use the example of one of my clients, a large technology company in the Silicon Valley area. Several years ago, they carved out and divested a product line and sold it to a private equity company. The company created a new business. The new company then became an entity as a divested unit.

I get excited about mergers, acquisitions, and divestitures, it's where I cut my teeth in negotiation. I've spent a fair amount of time in those types of deals, working in those companies, going through and experiencing those situations. The big thing, especially in a divestiture, is from a contractual perspective there is usually a change in the formal contracts that are in place with customers and suppliers. Those original contracts need to be able to be migrated to the new entity. There is much work involved in getting permissions to transfer contracts to the new entity. Sometimes contracts have standard language around transfer that makes it so that it's not allowed, or you have to have written permission. The other company in the contract may veto it. You need to take all of those kinds of things into account. So that's dependent on the style of the language in the formal agreement between the two parties.

Being the 'David' in the David and Goliath scenario, the most important thing to remember is - research.

I will continue to say throughout the rest of this book - your knowledge of yourself, your business, and your detailed researched understanding of your counterpart are your friend in these situations.

In a divestiture, if it's a big company, divesting a business, you get a lot of "we can't", "I won't", "we won't", "we're not able to", statements. They're not often true. If you are a large company and are divesting a business or product line, it's a lot of work.

I've had the pleasure of working on several divestitures. There is a lot of work involved in the contract side, and the business relationship going forward. There's just a lot of detail work that needs to get done, a lot of tracking work. There are organizations, consulting firms, and law firms that help companies to do that. You want to make sure that you have some rights included in your contract's transfer language. We will discuss contracts in greater detail in Part III, and get into some easy things to think about contractually. Things that can help you understand what you should focus on, whether in a diverse divestiture environment or not.


## MERGERS

A merger is when two somewhat similar companies, often termed mergers of equals, come together to create a new entity. You can have an acquisition, where a company is buying or absorbing another company's operations. That's the easiest way to think about it. You often see large companies acquiring smaller businesses.

Google is an acquisition machine. Juniper Networks is an acquisition machine. Cisco. Microsoft. Big consumer products. Companies like General Mills. The list goes on.

I used to say that some tech companies, particularly because I was working heavily in tech, were no longer technology companies. They were acquisition companies. They let smaller businesses develop, create, and innovate. Then they buy, absorb, and incorporate them into their overall offering. It's less expensive for them than doing that work.

Part of that is because it is a big company; if it's a publicly-traded company, they have earnings obligations that they have to hit. The second reason is that when you're doing a great deal of innovation, it's expensive and not profitable, which hurts their earnings expectation, and causes them to take a hit on their stock. So, they let smaller companies do the innovation and development because the smaller company doesn't have obligations of proving earnings to Wall Street. It's just much better business for the larger company to come in to buy them.

## ACQUISITIONS

If a Goliath company like Google, or Microsoft, (or take your pick of a Goliath company in your sector) is approaching you offering to buy your business, do not accept that first offer.

There's definitely something going on. You need to understand why. What is it that your business has to offer this big company?

There's something that you're doing that is appealing to them. They're not offering you money to buy you out of the goodness of their heart. It's because they think that there's a significantly greater return than the amount of money they are offering you. Just as in any other negotiation, you need to understand what their motivation is in courting you.

We often talk in the mergers and acquisitions world (m&a in industry lingo), in dating terms. If they're courting you and trying to buy you, there's a rationale for doing that.

Suppose a company approaches you to buy your business. In that case, you want to make sure you have a valuation done on your business. There are many different companies that help small businesses find buyers.

If you are looking to sell, and nobody's approached you, there are business brokers that will help you find potential buyers for your business. You want to have somebody who helps you through that process. Business owners do not generally think about themselves in terms of valuation. There are a lot of different methodologies and approaches to how you consider valuation. There are profound and intense books with lots of detail on how to think about a business' valuation. You want to make sure that you're getting a good value for your company and make sure that some things that are sacred to you in your business culture get protected.

Suppose you're a small business and have employees who have been with you for a long time. In that case, you may want to make sure that you protect your employees in the acquisition process. It's not just about how much money you're going to get.

How are they going to treat your customers?

If you've got long relationships with your customers, you want to make sure to safeguard them. You've built this business and protected it. You've birthed this thing into the market. You watched it grow. You want to make sure that what you've developed and what you've grown and built will survive and that it's not going to be, for lack of a better term, bastardized by the big company. Ultimately, it will change once it's acquired, but there are things that you want to think about in terms of what's important to you in a buyer.

Be intentional about it and think about it so that they won't sway you so easily. Just because somebody comes in, throws some cash on the table, doesn't mean you should accept the first offer.

That kind of situation is rare.

Usually, what happens is that as a small business, you decide that you want not to be operating your company anymore. You may have a family, you may have children who you want to spend time with. Or, you may have older children who do not want to inherit the business, as much as you want them to take it over. It is a growing issue for a lot of small businesses in the United States today.

There are many family-owned businesses, but the kids don't want anything to do with them.

Then what do you do?

You need to find a way of exiting that business, finding a way to sell it. There's a process you need to think about, everything from how you protect it when you sell it, to how to get this big chunk of cash in for the sale of the business.

And then you have all the other things to consider beyond that.

Are you set up to manage the tax deferments on that?

Do you have assets you want to cash out?

Do you have liabilities you're still paying?

You want to look for people whose business is to help you pay as little tax as you can on the proceeds from the sale of that business. You want to find somebody to advocate for you to ensure that the business's financial aspects are working. That the value you're getting paid is commensurate with the value you've created in the company through a business broker. Those are some of the things you need to think about if you decide to sell a business.

Conversely, let's say you are choosing to buy a business. In that case, you need to be very intentional about knowing what you want out of a company. You need to understand why you want it and how you expect the previous owner to stay involved in it or not.

There are just many parameters, whether it's a Goliath buying your company or another small business owner buying your company to consider. Be focused, intentional, and specific in your goals, no matter who may buy the business.

## PROFIT POTENTIAL

Profit potentials exist all the time, especially in the tech space. For instance, Uber and Lyft have not made a profit to save a soul.

In spite of that, their stock is doing just fine. Their financials, quite frankly, don't look very good in most cases.

When you're looking at possible investors, different types of investors come into play. When you're first starting, usually you will find family and friends as your early investors. You get those investors who help you build the business, who give you the money to build the company, but they're not operationally involved.

Then you move from that to angel investors, which tend to be high worth individuals who love making a bet by putting their money with small businesses. They often invest in a small number of companies. They usually have precise criteria that they need to see to make that investment. The numbers aren't one of them, because the company is not likely making money yet, everything is cost.

Usually, at that stage, somebody is making a significant investment in the management, management's idea, and how they see that business running. Once you have angel investors, and you go into the venture capital world. Early-stage venture capital still has a strong focus on the individual leading the business on the business strategy and the approach and what the idea is and market potential.

As you get into later-stage funding with a venture capitalist, you will have stages of involvement. It would be best to have an exit strategy because all those people don't want to be involved in your business long term. They are looking to get their money out.

Those companies usually exit by going public or selling to a

Goliath. As you move further into your investment cycle, your numbers need to start to be there, generally.

Clearly, there are outliers to this strategy. We've seen it with Uber and Lyft. It all depends on what the market is and what the business is.

## VENTURE CAPITALISTS

Venture capitalists are companies or businesses that invest in smaller *Startup* organizations. They often invest in the pharmaceutical industry, medical devices, and technology, there are venture capitalists in many different industries.

M any times, entrepreneurs of small *Startup* companies, or investment ideas, get intimidated by the large vision that a venture capitalist sees. The new business owner, who's just starting out, is often thinking small.

We all get locked into our own vision. We see something as it is, and we aren't necessarily able to see the big picture. When somebody else comes in and sees that big picture, it's almost like a reminder that we're thinking small, and it scares the daylights out of us. So, we put the brakes on.

You have this idea of what your business is going to be, you've got your vision. You've got this laid out, and you may have a three to five-year plan. If you're good at your business, you should have a three to five-year plan. Because most small business owners don't. They just kind of let the wind take them where it goes.

In this case, you had this kind of a narrow vision, and the wind blew in and brought this big landscape to you. And, you looked across that landscape and went, "Oh, hell no. I'm retreating to my comfortable little spot. And I'm going to go with what my comfortable little spot is telling me to do."

In that regard, it's all about one understanding;

What's driving that reaction?

Is it just a fear-based reaction?

Assess then, is the vision that the person just shared with me, that thing that they just showed me that I hadn't seen before?

Is it possible?

Is it a vision that I can, instead of just reacting and recoiling from it, explore it, play with it a little?

Think about it?

What is it?

What would it mean if that were to happen?

What would it look like, and how would I see that unfolding?

What might I need to make it happen?

What do I not have in or where my limitations were?

I might not have the capital or the skill set to bring that to fruition. What does that mean?

Does that mean that I have to give up control?

Because, if you get funding from a venture capitalist or an angel investor, you are giving up some of your business' control.

They're buying a stake; they're buying a percentage of your company, so you're absolutely giving something up to get that money. It's not like they're just giving you money, and they get nothing out of it. They get some ownership in your company, depending on how much they are investing.

You have to take that step back and take more of an objective view of it, research and go back into that analysis to say, "Well, wait, wait, I hadn't thought about that. I know what my vision is; it's over here. And there's this big thing. Is there a way of bridging? Is that possible?"

You don't shut the opportunity down out of the starting gate. Honor yourself by being willing to explore what that might be. To put some significant thought into whether or not it's something that you want to do. You're making a big decision. One not just based on the emotional reaction, but an informed decision about whether or not that's something in the realm of possibility for you as the owner of the business.

## ON PARTNERS

I'm often asked whether it's preferable to have a partner, instead of a venture capitalist.

That depends on how much the partner owns, or what you want. You can have a partner who has 2% of your company, have a partner who's an equal partner, or have a partner who owns 50% plus one share of a company.

They might have operational ownership and can hold all the major key deals. There are so many ways of structuring a partnership. You can have a partnership that's a joint venture, that's two separate companies working together that focus just on marketing, some specific activity, or product. You could have a development thing where you're doing r&d together. You can have revenue sharing or referral base things. There are so many different ways of structuring a partnership.

That's something that a lawyer is crucial in helping you do. They can help figure out, given your business, your objectives, and the right business structure for you as a company.

Also, if you are going to be partnering, what's the best partnering structure?

What's that entity kind of look like?

How does that relationship kind of work?

What makes the most sense?

Do you do a licensing model or franchising?

Do you do partners?

Affiliates?

What does that look like?

An attorney can give you some great advice on how that should be structured. They're not necessarily going to be good at telling you how to operationalize it. That's part of the partnering contract that comes into play. They definitely can say, "this is the kind of deal that makes the most sense."

A Goliath will already understand that as they have many gifted and knowledgeable attorneys who are well trained in those areas. When you're working with a Goliath, they're likely to provide you a copy of their contracts to start.

## ON FOUNDERS

I think that founders are interesting. As a founder of my own company, I find that founders are a fascinating breed.

Steve Jobs got fired from Apple. Then he came back and turned that company into what it is today. I don't know that this is necessarily about contracts as much as it is about how we are as individuals in our business.

When I was a career advisor at Harvard Business School, I worked with both students and the executive education program, and I learned many things.

One of the things I observed was that people who are good at starting something are not necessarily good at growing it. They're not necessarily good at maintaining that, and they're not necessarily good at winding it down.

My observation was that people tend to be good at maybe two of those things, but not all four of them. It stands to reason that a founder is good at getting it started and possibly really good at growing it.

Often a founder is not quite so good once it's hit a particular trajectory in its growth. Now it needs more structure, more organization, and more definitive processes to operate, to be successful. Now, it's a different personality type that comes into play, rather than someone flying by the seat of their pants, wearing all the hats.

Even when I was working in a tech *Startup*, as we grew, one of my other observations is that you'd go into a *Startup*, and you'd have a big title and a big piece of the pie.

But then, over time, as you got more and more people, your title started to shrink. Even if you kept the title, your slice of the pie got much smaller. You move from this generalist model into the specialist model. And generalists don't always morph well into that specialist world. When you have specialists, you have much more detail in structure and process, and format. How you do things becomes more regimented. It needs to be easily trainable and transferable.

You don't have that so much. When you're earlier, you're doing that whole general thing and doing all sorts of things.

When you're a small business owner, who also happens to be a founder, and your business starts to grow, make sure you have an exit strategy. I always encourage small business owners to have two exit strategies; one for their business - are they selling their business? Are they taking it public? What are they doing with the company? The second exit strategy is for themselves. They may have an exit strategy that's different from the business. Many people don't think far enough in advance to get that point.

One of the things I learned when I was doing a lot of career advising is that many people talk about the importance of vision. It is essential. Small business owners need to have a sense of that vision when they're starting out. If you don't know where you're trying to go, it will negatively impact your negotiations. You won't be able to find consistency in some of the things you need to get there.

One of the problems with vision is that some people are good at closing their eyes to see the 5-year vision, or the 1-year vision.

They don't think in 10-year, 20-year increments. Some people can't think out that far because not everybody's brain thinks that way.

Suppose you're somebody who focuses on a shorter-term vision. In that case, I encourage you to consider surrounding yourself with people who can help you think about what that longer-term view might look like. You need a longer-term view to get buy-in and confidence from your support and staff to create that momentum to carry you forward as your business grows.

## BOARD OF DIRECTORS

Whenever you're getting investors coming in and building a board of directors, there are contracts for each deal. A founder can work protections into those contracts, whether it's an angel investor or venture capitalists, or private equity. Private equity is different from venture capitalists who invest in newer companies and help companies grow. They then sell to take advantage of the benefits of what happened during that growth period.

To be clear on what private equity is, private equity usually comes in and buys a company that's in trouble. Then they rework the structure of the business entirely. They get rid of people and cut costs because they make money off of the improvement. There's a different mindset that goes with private equity to venture capital.

In all of those relationships, if you're a small business owner seeking investors, then you will have contracts related to those investors. If a private equity firm is interested in acquiring your company, there will be contracts related to that. You want to be able to do many things to maintain how you're involved in the organization. It depends on which side of that you are on and how successful the business is. If the company's not doing well, you're not likely to have much influence over a long period. But, they still may want to have you stay there for some level of continuity for a while. To be able to maintain morale within the organization. But it all varies, again, no different than any other negotiation. If you are looking at investors, you need to know what you want, why you want it, figure out your trade-offs. You need to anticipate how what you want will impact your counterpart and what that impact will have on your investor. Investor negotiations follow the same process as every other negotiation.

## TRACY'S TOYS AND TARGET

Here's an example of a David and Goliath story. Let's say there is an independent toy store in a rural part of the United States. Let's call that store – Tracy's Toys, owned by a woman named Tracy.

In Tracy's store, there are approximately 9000 SKUs. SKUs, for those not familiar, are stock-keeping units.

Every product has a unique code to track inventory; SKUs are individual numbers associated with a product. They have 9000 SKUs in this small retail store in rural America.

Tracy has these products that suddenly become a big hit, and she must buy these particular products through a distributor.

Because she's small, she can't afford to buy as much as a Target or a Walmart can. The one benefit she has is that she can access the product before it moves into Target and Walmart's supply chain.

Tracy was able to get this particular "hot" product on her shelves. She was able to order three cases. Two of the cases, she was able to sell before they hit Walmart and Target because she got them two months ahead of those two companies. She was able to sell them at a higher price because they weren't in the big box retail stores yet.

However, once they hit Walmart and Target, it's at this insanely low price, a price that she cannot compete with.

Target and Walmart sell at a lower price than Tracy can

purchase them from her distributor because she also has to pay astronomical shipping costs.

So, now she just got her third case of this product, but she can't sell it.

If she were trying to sell it now, she'd have to sell it at a loss. Her solution was to go to her local big-box retailers and buy all their product. She's buying it up to make more money by selling it closer to the holiday season because it'll be a big seller for her during the holiday season.

Tracy creates scarcity by buying that product; she's buying it at a lower cost by buying it from the retailer than buying from the distributor. Because she made enough profit off the first two cases, she can now hold that third case and acquire more inventory from Target or Walmart. She can acquire that inventory and then sell it at a higher margin further into the holiday season.


## SMALL BUSINESS OWNERS

As for small business owners, it feels like there's one barrier after another after another. As I'm getting ready to launch my podcast, I had an interesting conversation with one gentleman I'm going to be interviewing. He's the third-generation owner of a family electrical business in Oklahoma. Regulation kills him compared to more prominent companies because he has a smaller population to put the costs across. He has a smaller amount of revenue to absorb that cost related to staying compliant with the regulations. We've got regulations, and we have taxes, and we've got this, and we've got that.

For small business owners to be successful, they have to get super creative sometimes, which is advantageous to you, as a small business owner, when negotiating with a Goliath. Your ability to be flexible is a huge advantage. A Goliath company takes forever to change a simple process; when they have to get who knows how many people signing off on it. If you want to do something that's not in their standard contract, it's like pulling teeth to get it done. But you, as a small business owner, are nimble. You need to leverage that nimbleness in your relationships, especially with a more prominent company or a company you see as having more power and influence than you do. Because your ability to be creative will allow you to find ways of creating value for yourself, and it might also create additional value for your counterpart.

This is why listening with intent, which we talked about just a little bit ago in the book, is critical.

The research is also essential because the amount of money you can make from your customers is more. The amount that you spend with your suppliers is less, and the value that you're creating for yourself by doing those things becomes very tangible in David and Goliath negotiation.

## BIG BOX COMPANIES

There is one particular Big Box company that has a reputation for being impossible to negotiate with. They have historically had a policy where they share very little information and are very demanding. You go in; you sit in a tiny room with the buyer, their negotiator. It's pretty much them just dictating to you what the situation is going to be - how much they're going to buy, and how much they're willing to pay per unit for what they're buying.

They have a policy of changing out the negotiator that you're dealing with regularly so that there is a revolving door of buyers. So, in a two-year relationship, you might have dealt with at least two if not three or four different buyers of that product.

This company does not necessarily have a high turnover in that role. There have been stories and Harvard business cases written about this company. Most salespeople hate dealing with this company so much. They hate them so much because it's so defeating to go in and just be told, "it's our way or the highway."

In contrast, I met this guy once. He is a fantastic negotiator. When we started talking about this, this organization, he got so excited. I was shocked when he proclaimed, "I love negotiating with them." I was inquisitive about that because everybody else I'd ever talked to who had negotiated with them did not like to deal with them.

"What is it that you love so much?" I asked.

"I have such an advantage as a small business negotiating with them. They lose the history of our relationship every time they switch out to a new buyer.", he responded, "I have figured out how to leverage that, I have figured out how to make the most out of that because I am nimble and they are not. Because they lose that history of all the things we've discussed, there are things that I can bring back up into the negotiation with this new person, that works to my benefit."

This is a great example of a "David" that found creative ways to negotiate with a "Goliath" of a company.

## GROUP ADVISORS

Having a group of advisors that you can connect to, who can help push your thinking is essential. As a Startup, you might feel 'advisory board' seems like a Goliath term, yet there are benefits to starting small with a mastermind group.

We're all limited in how we think about a situation. Our past experiences inform our thinking about a specific situation. That automatically makes us myopic or singularly focused on how we view our world. For me, it's about making sure that I've got other people who think differently than I do. People who aren't there to pat me on the back and say, "Way to go, keep going, you're doing great."

I also want somebody who will push me and challenge me

and ask me hard questions. Someone who will show me things, put a mirror in front of my face to say, "Do you see what you're doing?" So that I can find ways of moving beyond where I'm stuck if I am stuck.

It's also about this lifelong learning aspect, reading story after story about small business owners. I feel like every small business owner should have a book, which is one reason I'm so excited about my podcast, "In the Venn Zone." The show is about all things negotiation. I have guests who talk about respect at the negotiation table, a mom who talks about standing in her strength while buying a company and nursing during the negotiation, a rancher who teaches riding lessons and talks about moving people incrementally through the change process and knowing one's value. There are CEOs and everyday people sharing their stories of negotiation.

Part of what has helped me in my negotiation and being creative is that I have negotiated across many different industries. It taught me to see parallels and how things in the financial sector can be related to the oil and gas industry and then connected to the pharmaceutical industry. I can see where there's some overlap. That's not necessarily overlapping operations, but how we can think through a problem differently. A solution that may have worked in the oil and gas industry may be similar to what's happening in this financial services company.

That's why I'm so excited about the podcast. My intention was to create something will be easily accessible for small businesses to learn these different styles and techniques to apply to their own business.

## WHEN TO BRING IN A NEGOTIATOR

Suppose you're a small business owner, and you are going into a David and Goliath negotiation. In that case, they will probably have multiple people in that conversation to your one person.

In a case like that, I would encourage you not to bring an attorney until deep into the process. You want to time that very carefully because as soon as you have an attorney, they have to have an attorney. There's a whole process.

If I'm negotiating with somebody, and they tell me that they have a negotiation going on right now, with a landlord, who also happens to be an attorney, I disclose that I am not an attorney. Then they, knowing that I'm not an attorney, know that I'm not approaching the negotiation from a legal perspective. It changes the dynamic some.

Try to avoid bringing an attorney into that discussion. You could get somebody from your advisory board or one of your staff to be in that negotiation with you. I would encourage you to at least have a second person in a David and Goliath negotiation. You must have somebody taking notes. It would be best if you were listening, but you need to have somebody taking notes. They have 3, 4, or 5 people listening to the same conversation, which means that they have 6, 8, or 10 ears picking up on different aspects of that conversation. That is valuable information because they will leave that meeting and they will debrief.

If it's just you, you don't pick up anything. You will only hear what you hear. The problem with that is, you will often listen to what you want to hear. Having a second party in that meeting with you is vital, whether it's somebody like me who is a professional negotiator or somebody on your staff who's just taking notes.

Before you go into the meeting, you want to do all the things we've talked about already. You want to be prepared. You want to have researched. Before you get to that meeting, make sure you ask who will be in attendance at the meeting. Know who's going to be at that meeting and research them. Figure out who these people are, how do they think, what's important to them? What do they like to do? It is essential, so you have something to deal with and to talk about from an icebreaker perspective.

Make sure you have an agenda; make sure you know exactly what you will be talking about. So set the plan, you send them a draft agenda of what you want to discuss. Let them know that if they have any additions to the agenda, they can feel free to send them back to you.

Make sure that you are controlling the agenda. Write it on the whiteboard, or make sure everybody has a copy of it when they're sitting down.

That's a way for you to maintain control. It's a small thing; but it is a big thing.

It gives you some leverage in the negotiation because now you look like you're commanding the conversation. You're taking ownership of that conversation.

It's a solid, effective tool, especially in a David and Goliath negotiation.

When the meeting is over, and you've gone through the agenda, take the notes and clean them up neat, structured, and formatted, so they align to the agenda.

Then you send the notes to your counterparts, and you say, "these are the notes from the meeting, please let us know if we missed anything, please add to them." Then those notes become a document of record that you can reference.

I like to keep track of things agreed to, open and unresolved things that have been discussed, and things that have not yet been discussed. That gives you a running tally so that you're tracking all the small wins upfront, all the wins. You want to keep track of all those wins, one so that you don't go back and renegotiate them unless there's a good reason to do so. You also want to be able to communicate, "look at all the things we talked about, 20 different items. We've reached agreement in principle on 16 of them. So, there are only four things in today's conversation that are still open that we don't have agreement on."

I always use the term "agreement in principle" when I'm at meetings, if their attorney is not involved. Once attorneys get involved, just because you have an agreement in principle, it doesn't necessarily mean that it will stay that way.

I n the next chapter, we're going to be talking about needing to know when to disengage. Knowing when to walk away from a negotiation is one of the ultimate power tools in a negotiation.

# 8

# ON WHEN TO DISENGAGE AND WALK AWAY

*A boiling teapot eventually runs out of steam.*

I think people tend to stay too late in a negotiation that isn't working. In Chapter 4, I talked about the power of the full stop sentence, and how important those two little letters 'N' and 'O,' can be.

The thing is, many times people get into this mentality in negotiations and will say - I have to close this deal.

Especially feeding off the previous chapter, with David and Goliath negotiations. It goes towards people's motivations and why they do things.

As soon as you convince yourself that you must close a deal, you have put yourself in an unfavorable position for advocating for what you want. You can be too focused on closing the final deal, overlooking the pieces and parts that are a component of that overall deal.

In my experience, people often enter into contracts when they should have probably walked away. It can be because the person they're negotiating with was being a bully. It could also be because they failed to see how negatively a point they ended up agreeing to would impact their business. That could happen, mostly if they were not prepared enough. They've not articulated clearly what their goals and objectives are from the negotiation. They don't understand the impact a proposal may have on their overall business.

When that happens, they often find reasons to live with a deal that's not in their best interest instead of walking away from that deal.

## WHEN THINGS GO SOUTH

Often, when a business negotiation goes south, there are a couple of different scenarios.

For me, one scenario is that my counterpart gets so angry that they walk out of the room, and out of the negotiation. If my counterpart were to do that with me, I would set some terms under which I would allow that person to come back into the negotiation. That raises a whole bunch of alarm bells for me in terms of what that person will be like once the deal gets finalized. And suppose that's how they're going to behave while we're negotiating. In that case, I'm pretty concerned about how they're going to behave once the negotiation is finished. So, I might decide to allow somebody to come back into a negotiation if they have stormed out. But I also may decide that that's the end of the negotiation. I don't want to continue to do business with that person, given that reaction. Now that decision is 100% on me whether I reengage with that individual or not.

The second situation, is where somebody has entered into a negotiation, signed a deal, and it's agreed. This is where you get some legal aspects that come back into things. Lawyers may have a different view than what I might share because they'll take a very legal perspective on what's doable and not. In contrast, I'm taking more of a pragmatic view that is not rooted in law since I'm not an attorney. From a pragmatic perspective, how recently you've renegotiated or negotiated a deal will likely impact whether or not you can renegotiate it.

In Part III of this book, we're going to go into a lot more detail about renegotiation. It's a topic I'm pretty passionate about. Renegotiation has to be part of the sales strategy from the beginning if we embrace the concept of a lifetime customer. Your ability to renegotiate is driven by some of the factors we're going to talk about later. If you've recently entered into a deal, then it's much harder; it's going to be harder for you to renegotiate it if it's a brand-new deal. That doesn't mean that it's not possible; you have to be transparent with your counterpart and admit that something has changed.

Maybe it's an external factor that influences your ability to adhere to that; perhaps there was a chain reaction component. Say you had a deal that relied on two other contracts going through, and you did not bake in a contingency into the contract with your customer. So now that one of those two deals didn't happen, and you can't deliver, as you committed to. You could go back to your counterpart and say, "I thought this was going to happen, and it didn't. It is going to affect our ability to deliver."

There are lots of times when you have situations where people have entered into agreements. Perhaps their ability to deliver is hampered by some external factor or even an internal factor. Maybe it's a piece of software, and something happened during its development. And it hasn't been able to pass through its testing the way somebody believed that it was going to when they sold it to you. Generally speaking, if you've got a situation where there's something that your ability to perform against the contract is contingent upon, you want to include that in a deal.

This contingency clause addresses that upfront, you want to be able to say upfront to your counterpart – "I'm selling you this, and you're buying this, but you have to understand that these other things have to be in place for me to deliver it. If those things are delayed, it will impact my ability to deliver to you."

My recommendation is, if you know that's a situation, then you should be disclosing that in the negotiation process, long before you sign an agreement.

If I'm in the negotiation, I'm not likely to be open to negotiating or renegotiating a recently signed contract. Not unless there is significant evidence that performing the contract will cause extreme damage to my counterpart. I'll sit and say, "Why wasn't this disclosed upfront? You should have known this upfront and should have let me know upfront. Now, this is going to cause me damages."

It's essential to think about the things that could impact your ability to perform and deliver. Be transparent about them, be upfront about it, because it'll save you time, money, potentially a lost customer, and lawsuits if you are upfront and transparent versus not.

# PART III

## MAKING THE DEAL WORK

# 9

# GETTING WHAT YOU WANT

*Be curious about yourself, your counterpart, and the situation you are negotiating.*

W e've covered a lot of ground to get here.
We started with the first key - Effective Preparation, know what you want and why you want it. Then we went to a second key, Successful Engagement, how to ask for what you want.

Now we're at the third key, Making the Deal Work. This is the essential step to ensure you're getting what you agreed upon with your counterpart. In this chapter, we're going to discuss contracts and risk management in regard to contracts.

## INFORMAL CONTRACTS

Earlier in the book, I mentioned there are two kinds of contracts - formal and informal. Many people, when they hear the words "informal contract", get a bit of a red flag.

I often get asked - don't we all have to have formal contracts? If we don't have it, then is the contract binding?

Do we then need proof and evidence of it?

All kinds of alarms go off when you talk about informal contracts.

The reality is, informal contracts are very, very common. Anecdotally, I expect that more deals are informal than formal. Informal contracts can be contracts that you wrote on the back of an envelope or a napkin. It could be something you agreed and threw into a text. Or you shot an email over to somebody, or they're done just verbally on a handshake.

Those are still legally binding agreements. They're obligations that you still have to adhere to. But you do need to maintain proof of what those relationships entail.

One of the big problems, especially with verbal negotiation, or agreement, is that people don't remember things the same way.

Just ask my mom; the things that she recalls from my childhood are not the same as I remember. She'll often say, "That's not what happened.", to which I'll respond, "Yes it is!"

Imagine trying to take that into a business. It becomes challenging because you just don't remember things the same way. Two people can simultaneously look at the same object and see two different things because we focus on different things. Suppose you don't have things documented if you're doing a handshake agreement, or whatever the informal agreement structure is. When you don't have some level of documentation, it opens you up to risk and the possibility that that agreement is not honored on one side or the other.

## FORMAL CONTRACTS

People think of formal contracts because most people don't think of a handshake or what you agreed to do on the napkin as being a contract. As soon as they think of contracts, people's eyes glaze over. They think of an attorney and that an attorney is the only one on the planet who can negotiate a contract.

You get this elite-ism as far as what a contract is, and who's allowed to do something with them. But the reality is, over 70% of major corporations give contract-related work to non-attorneys. So only 30% of corporate contracting related work is done by lawyers.

People often do it in procurement, contract management, sales, and different departments where contracts come into play. Attorneys in major corporations usually come into the contracting process at the end. Not when I'm negotiating, I try to bring them in sooner to get the terms and conditions of the contract spelled out before we negotiate price, as I've mentioned before.

In many cases, most corporations' processes are that a salesperson sells to their company and the business owner. Then the business owner engages with procurement. They will get the deal to a certain point; they do the bulk of the contract work. Right before it needs to have final approval, they throw it over the wall to the lawyer, and then the lawyer shreds the whole thing. They come back with all these red lines and say that's not going to work. It's often the attorney just putting their stamp of authority on it. It is why a deal is never done until it's actually closed.

You'll hear people talk about, especially in sales, as an 80% probability, it's going to close. Until it's a signed contract, it is not done, in my book.

Contracts are binary; they're done and signed, or they're not. There's nothing in the middle.

. . .

W hen working with a significant company, you can expect them to have a contract and have a standard agreement. They will initiate the use of their understanding in a negotiation kind of language or parlance; it's called using their paper. When you hear somebody say, "It's on our paper," it means that they wrote the initial contract. That's going to be the starting point.

I prefer not to say "my" paper or "their" paper; I call it the origin point. Because at the end of the day, the contracts are agreed upon by both parties.

There is a big discussion, and academics will tell you that it matters a lot whether you're originating the contract or whether the counterpart is originating the contract. And that's true to a point because you have anchoring that happens. Anchoring is when you put it in somebody's mind, and then they kind of fix it. That's the starting point, then they don't go backward from that necessarily as quickly once they see it in writing.

Having an understanding of the different contract types is vital. Small business owners need to understand that just because it's a formal contract, it doesn't mean you should be abdicating that document to your attorney. Because at the end of the day, contracts serve one primary function, and that is that they are risk mitigation tools.

Contracts are the documents that, when you've gone through your negotiation, and you've completed it, that essentially codifies or puts into history how the relationship is supposed to work over time.

My lawyer friends may disagree with me. While a contract is a risk mitigation tool, it is a document based on the hope of a positive future and a mutually beneficial relationship in the future. Many people look at a contract, and they look at it with absolute dread and loathing. The language is complicated and annoying because who uses "Legal-ese" like that in daily language, except for attorneys? Nobody.

That's intimidating language for people. In reality, you can strip a lot of that stuff away and just get to the essential parts of the contract. The thing is, is that they're simply risk mitigation tools.

## RISK MITIGATION

There are five types of risks within a contract, whether it's formal or informal. Keep in mind that regardless of whether it's formal or informal, a contract's primary purpose is risk mitigation.

Risk mitigation applies to both of those types of contracts in all five of these different risk categories.

The first risk is cash flow risk. Cash flow risk is often laid out in a contract based on things like payment terms. An obvious thing that people think about there are payment terms. There's a penalty for late payment. There might be a benefit if you pay early. There's a percentage rate perhaps included in the contract for late payment. But that's all in. That's how that gets defined in terms of one of the aspects of cash flow in the contract.

I had a client one time during the dot-com bubble bursting, that was a product merchandising company. They put your logo on coffee mugs, tote bags, and all those kinds of things. The majority of their customers were technology companies, and that market was shrinking dramatically. The number of customers they had was diminishing. The amount of money each of those customers was spending was also decreasing. They had this massive customer - a very well-known carbonated beverage company. This large customer was taking 180 days to pay them, which was a common tactic. For my customer to be able stay in business and keep paying their employees, we had to figure out how to get that big beverage company to pay faster. We did all sorts of things. We put forward a cash flow discussion. We were able to secure a new contract with them based on accelerating that cash flow position.

That's an example of how cash flow can play out in contract terms. It's also an easy one for people to wrap their head around because it's money based. When we think about our business relationships, we often drop down to the dollar. When we see dollar amounts or a percentage, some mathematical representation of the deal, we tend to focus on that in a document.

Cash flow is absolutely a thing that an element of risk that gets managed in the contract.

The second one is profitability. Profitability is not necessarily as easy to measure because it's tied to many things in the contract. I was negotiating a deal with a large insurance company. They were buying software that my client was offering. It was one of those deals that the salesperson had waited to the last possible moment of the quarter, which also happened to be the end of the year, to push forward this deal. And this is a trick that people do all the time. They wait until the very last part of the last week of a quarter to move things because they think you're motivated to get something done, and that could be the case. If you can, don't buy into that trick. Try to do all the things that we've talked about in terms of preparation, due diligence, and understanding, so you don't become a victim of that unnecessary timing component.

In this particular case, the company had added language into the contract that would require my client to increase to a new level of insurance. They needed to add insurance that they didn't already have, and they had to increase their insured levels.

The sales team had already "agreed to price" - it's set in stone.

I called my client's insurance company, and asked "How much is it going to cost us to add this insurance?"

It was a significantly different policy and considerably higher levels of insurance than we currently had. It was going to cost us $60,000 a year. On a $100,000 deal, that's profitability. This is one reason I don't like to negotiate the price ahead of negotiating the contract if it's something like that that sits into that contract. That's an example of how profitability can come into play.

The third risk is operational risk. Let's say that you are a manufacturer. You have a product, but you contract out to another manufacturer, who holds inventory for you on your behalf and ships it to your customers.

Let's say something happens to that manufacturer and they can no longer hold inventory. Now, operationally, you have to make some changes. You have to figure out how to move that product from that manufacturer to a different manufacturer if you decide to do that.

Are you going to move it to you?

Are you going to manage your inventory yourself?

If you're going to manage your inventory, what kind of people and resources do you need?

If you're going to manage inventory, what type of space do you need?

How long are you going to hold that?

What does it look like on your balance sheet because now you have finished goods inventory sitting in your property?

It has a substantial operational impact on your business.

Understanding what the terms and conditions are in a contract helps, operationally, as you have to comply with for that contract.

. . .

The fourth risk mitigation is strategic. For strategic risk, I'll use a software example. Software companies are easy ones for me to explain from a strategy perspective. Software companies have development roadmaps. They map out what features and benefits they will release on those roadmaps, which can cover three to five years of development.

Sometimes you get a customer who requires a certain benefit or feature that you're going to roll out in two years – but they want it now. What does that mean? That software roadmap drives every aspect of work that happens in a tech company, in a software company.

If I move that feature up two years, what do I have to do to make that happen?

There are operational implications to it for sure. Do I need to have additional resources?

Do I have to have new contracts with other third-party software vendors?

Do I do that development in parallel with my existing roadmap?

Or, do I take a feature off my roadmap now and delay it?

If I do that, what's the implication to my existing customer base?

What's the implication to revenue short term and long term?

If I bring that feature up and develop it early, is there a benefit to me regarding my revenue?

And, how does the cost often offset that?

That has a massive impact on the strategic direction of the company. That's a strategic risk that exists within the contract.

A note here about Goliaths. I often see Goliath organizations having the most destructive impact on smaller companies in this area of risk. It seems innocent enough. They ask you to develop a feature you hadn't planned. The sales team is telling engineering, "We have to do this in order keep the customer happy." And maybe they are right. See what's happening here? You're in the throes of a negotiation. Get prepared. Know your numbers. Honestly evaluate what you can and can't do and be transparent with your customer. Ask effective questions to discover what the customer really is trying to accomplish. I've seen too many companies jump through hoops to satisfy a Goliath only to find they've missed the mark or the need wasn't as great as the Goliath implied. They were just testing you. Stay curious at all times!

S o far, four of the five risk mitigation factors are business-related things. The last one is legal.

80% of the risk factors in a contract are business risks, not legal risks.

In California, where Venn Negotiation is headquartered, at the beginning of 2020, the California Legislature imposed what's called AB5. AB5 is a law that essentially makes all gig workers full employees.

Uber drivers, Doordash delivery people; under AB5, all of those people are to become full company employees. There are all sorts of reasons for this to make sense.

Now, Uber and Lyft are threatening to pull out of California if this law gets fully enacted. That law caused many companies to adjust contracts to address the fact that they cannot use contracted employees anymore.

That's an example of how law can drive a change or an aspect of risk or create new risk within your contracts and business relationships. People must understand that, again, 80% of the five primary risk factors are business-related risks. Yet, small businesses frequently get a contract from a company, and then they hand it off to their attorney. Their attorney doesn't know anything about those four other aspects of risk; they know the legal element of risk; their role is to keep you out of jail. They will frequently tell you that orange jumpsuits do not look good on you, and they don't. Their job is to make sure that what you're doing keeps you out of jail and limits your liability so you don't get sued or lose your company in the long term. As the business owner or entrepreneur, regarding cash flow, if you're going to be profitable or need to make operational or strategic changes to your business to accommodate the relationship, that's on you. You need to know that stuff.

One of the things we do in our live training programs is to take real contracts and teach people how to think through the different clauses and assign them to these five categories. Once you assign them to the five categories, if you have a clause that impacts all five of those things, you know that it's a clause that you need to renegotiate. You need to negotiate that language. Suppose it's a clause that hits cash-flow and profitability. In that case, you may decide profit matters more to you, or you could decide cash-flow matters more to you right now, so you will take a hit on profitability. It gives you a straightforward framework to evaluate what kind of risk you're trying to mitigate. It gives you a way of looking at that risk and figuring out how to prioritize the risk in the trade-offs as you're going through the actual contract.

# 10

# RENEGOTIATION

*Listen to what's being said in between the words. That is where
you'll find opportunities and potential.*

W hen you're at the end of a new negotiation, a new
relationship, or a new contract, you run into a new set
of risks. The thing is, those same risks that you're working to
mitigate in the contract also become the drivers for the need to
renegotiate.

It's generally because one of those five things is out of
whack. Maybe you're in a relationship, and the profitability you
thought would be there, has somehow been eroded.

It could be because your suppliers' cost may have increased,
and the cost that you're selling a product for no matter no longer
makes sense, you need to make some adjustments to that.

It could be that the profitability you had planned in the
contract doesn't exist anymore and might be driving you to need
to renegotiate.

If you have to go back, you can take each of these five risk
factors, and you can look at them as examples of how they can
drive the rationale for renegotiation.

With cash flow, that company that I was telling you about with that large beverage company was a renegotiation. We renegotiated that contract and took a hit on profitability in that renegotiation because we accelerated our delivery time.

We made some additional product changes for that client to get a different mix of products that they wanted. We offered at a lower price so that we could get that cash in much sooner. And we were able to reduce that payment cycle from 180 days down to 60 days. When you think about a hurting company where most of their customers are going out of business, their revenue opportunities are shrinking. Moving one large customer from paying in 180 days to paying in 60 days has a monumental impact on that business. That's an example of how cash flow is not only a risk factor but how that can drive a rationale for needing to renegotiate.

When it comes to profitability and renegotiation, I had a client that was a small software company; it was an internet services provider company. And they owed a legitimate liability to a large Goliath hosting services company. Essentially, the contract had eroded by that point. The liability was over a million dollars. The relationship had deteriorated to the point where the Goliath had sent my client a letter saying they were kicking them out of their data center. That essentially meant that they were going to go out of business. They didn't have the money to pay the million dollars plus liability.

On the surface, one would think this is a cash flow discussion. And it could have been, but the CEO of this company, Mr. David Steinberg, had terrific foresight. He was an incredible CEO. He knew that he did not need to focus on how bad the deal he had entered into was. Instead, he needed to focus on going forward and what the future would look like. He couldn't be stuck in the moment, looking at how bad things were with the dot-com bubble bursting. He said, "Christine, just take care of this." He was trying to get additional investors.

Cash flow can be a thing that investors care about, but profitability is absolutely something investors care about. His objective to get new investors into the company when people were not investing in tech companies meant that profitability was a huge issue.

We renegotiated a deal where we completely restructured that relationship. We extended the terms of the contract. We change the products we use. We educated people differently on how to use the products differently. We added some things and took some things out in terms of what we did with that particular supplier. Not only did we reduce that million-plus liability by 73%, but they also stayed in operation. They continued that relationship. that company stayed in existence for seven more years and sold for $123 million to a Fortune 500 company.

That's an example where profitability can drive the rationale for renegotiation.

It's important to understand that renegotiation is different from negotiation in a vital way in negotiation when you're all at the table. It's because you all have hope for positive benefits to come from the future of this relationship.

In a renegotiation for somebody at the table, that benefit does not exist. But just because the deal is not working for you does not mean it doesn't appear to be still working for your counterpart.

That's why these contract risks that you were mitigating in the negotiation process become the rationale for driving the need to renegotiate. You need a justification because your counterpart may not be seeing the same issues and problems with the deal as you are.

## RENEGOTIATING RATIONALE

Just like you have cash flow risk, you have cash flow as a rationale for renegotiating. Just like you have profitability risk, you have profitability as a rationale for renegotiation. If you have operational risk, you have operational issues as motivation for renegotiating.

Earlier in the book, I talked about a client and friend who has a machine shop. He had a pre-existing relationship with this behemoth company. He received a new contract saying he had to expedite 50%, but the customer was only going to guarantee 5% of that volume.

There's no way that he could do that with his 12 employees. How is he going to have the resources?

Is he going to hold raw material?

Is he going to hire and have it finished?

Is he going to bring in additional resources?

How is it going to get shipped?

Suppose he had been in a situation where it had been his contract already. If he had been one of those who had already signed that contract and couldn't deliver against the 50% expedited order, this operational aspect would be the rationale for driving that renegotiation.

Another example of a rationale for operational issues, I have been in situations where a company will come to me and say that they are changing their terms and conditions. They now require my client's HR team to do more background checks, drug testing, and all of that kind of stuff. We pushed back on that because that creates operational changes.

On the operational side, those Goliath companies will often include an overview of standard operating procedures. For example, you have to put a shipping label in this way. You have to invoice us in precisely this way, and if you deviate from this in any way, shape, or form, we don't have to pay you. Be very careful that you review. If that language is in a contract, make sure you review those documents to confirm that it is possible to do what those documents have said that you have to do. If you can't, negotiate it. If those things come up after you've entered into an agreement, use that as an opportunity to renegotiate because those have operational implications on your business.

Just like there is strategic risk that you're working to mitigate in the contract, there is a strategic rationale for renegotiation. That software example that I used before is a great example. Suppose you have a deal with a client already; you're already working under the terms of the agreement, and the customer comes back to you and says, I want that feature two years early. In that case, you need to evaluate whether that's doable. You have justify your ask because it will affect your business strategically.

Finally, you have legal renegotiation. You have a legal rationale for renegotiating, just like you're mitigating legal risk. AB5 in California is a situation that drove many companies to need to renegotiate some of their contracts. They needed to ensure that their staffing providers and other suppliers were being compliant with this new law.

One if not all of these five risk factors are prevalent or present in every deal, but your contracts are there to help mitigate that risk. Those same risk factors are what drive the need to renegotiate our contracts. When you need to enter into a renegotiation, being able to articulate the rationale for it within those risk components is helpful. When you're renegotiating, your objective is to convince your counterpart that it's in their best interest to renegotiate the deal.

These rationales provide you with more objectivity.

Urban Outfitters randomly decided they were going to quit playing their leases. Their reasoning was the COVID pandemic. While COVID is a reason, it is not a sufficient one. Companies like Regency Centers are suing Urban Outfitters because they decided to up and not to continue paying on their lease.

WeWork just quit paying their landlords. That doesn't do anything to build goodwill. You need to have some rationale that will cause somebody to want to work with you to help you prob-lem-solve that situation if you need to renegotiate.

It's about the relationship.


## PERFORMANCE REVIEW

I encourage people and companies to do a performance review of the contract pretty much annually, especially with key suppliers and customers. Am I giving you what I told you I would give you? Are you giving me what you told me you would provide to me? The give and the get. Is the 'give' right? And is the 'get' right?

If you don't create opportunities to have that kind of dialogue frequently when things start to go wrong and start to go off the rails, then people don't mention it. You don't have a way of observing it. You haven't created an environment or an opportu-nity to discuss it. Eventually, it will start to fester and build, creating a damaged relationship over time.

It's crucial that you try to spend at least once a year, once every other year, at minimum, to evaluate whether the deal is still working for the different parties.

Also, there have been many times when I walked into a company and saw contracts that were over 20 years old. Some of the contracts were 2-3000 pages of 20 years of documents.


N ot long ago, I was negotiating with a company with "Year 2000" language in their contract. Why is Y2K language in here right now? That was over 20 years ago.

There are so many things that change and business changes so fast in today's environment that I strongly encourage people to renegotiate contracts every five years. It keeps the contracts cleaner and makes them easier to follow. Because if you do have an old contract, and you just make amendment after amendment, and you make all these incremental changes to it, it ends up really confusing and frustrating. It's hard to manage that.

## RE-EVALUATE KPIS

Key Performance Indicators, or KPIs, are what you use when you sit down to do that annual or bi-annual review to ensure that your 'gives' and your 'gets' are right. It can be things around the timeliness of delivery or related to customer service and response times. It can be about failure rates, whether a product is defective or not.

How many defects are shipped in a product?

Or, are there installation issues?

There can be several different factors that go into play. That it depends on what business you're in, and what the contract is related to is what's going to drive what those KPIs are.

## TEMPLATES

When using pre-developed templates for different legal documents, organizations like LegalZoom and Legal Shield and attorneys will generally have template packages.

My biggest advice is to make sure that you're getting them from somebody reputable. It can be very beneficial to use a template. It's there because a lot of the legal language of contracts is relatively standard. Even if you're using a template document, you want to ensure that the document is still reflective of you and your business. Not every document should be the same. It's not one-size-fits-all, all of the time.

You want to be aware of what you're trying to get. It goes back to knowing what you want and why you want it because your standard terms and conditions should reflect them. That is what you're trying to create by using a template as a starting point.

For me, in my mind, that's precisely what they are. They're good starting points, but they're not always meant to be the final document you use. But it's a good starting point that you can add to, to include things that are important to you in your relationships and your business.

## PRODUCT OR SERVICE FAILURES

You typically address product and service failures in warranty sections of the contract, end-user support agreements, or other clauses in the main contract.

You can have a deal with a warranty that says how much product you're going to get, and how much failure you can expect to recover. If the number of defects or if the failure rate exceeds what was specified in the warranty, then there is a certain amount of money.

If you have a defective product that you have to replace, the cost of shipping is your responsibility. It depends on the defective product or what has failed and how important it is relative to the business.

You can figure out precisely what the remedy, another technical term, would be if a product fails and what the obligations are concerning the supplier of that particular product.

## NEGOTIATION FASCINATION

One of the things that's always really interesting about negotiating and renegotiating is that it's inherently individual. Each of us can be drawn to negotiate for the same thing, but still approach it in very, very different ways. And the things that are important to each of us as individuals vary. I think that for me, that's what I love about what I do. I can see that variability in people and see what drives us to make different decisions and behave in different ways in situations that appear to be similar. It is fascinating to me.

I was watching a program with procurement expert and president of ProPurchaser.com, Rod Sherkin. He talked about barbecues and steel price because, in charcoal grills, steel is a significant component.

Say you buy barbecues, and you retail them to the consumer. Then your supplier comes in and says the price of steel has gone up, we're going to raise the barbecues' price.

As the buyer of those barbecues, do you know what's been going on with steel prices? The price of steel may have gone up now. However, it still may be lower than when you entered into your buying contract with that particular supplier.

When you don't understand what's going into your products from your suppliers, you're leaving yourself open for risk and being taken advantage of. Especially if they just come in and tell you that because steel prices are going up; they have to jack up your prices.

A lot of small business owners might negotiate it, but they don't understand what's going on with the steel price.

That brings us right back to one of the key messages I shared at the beginning of the book -research, research, research.

## FINAL THOUGHTS

When I was about twenty, I came up with a quote that defines how I look at goals - "Put your goals in concrete, and your plans and sand."

When it comes to negotiation, know what it is that you want and why you want it. Once you know that, hold to that. Hold to what you want, that goal.

More is possible in your negotiation than you think.

In Chapter 3, I mentioned my adage - *if you can conceive it, you can paper it.*

If you can think about it, you can make it real; you can make it happen.

Who knew that flying jetpacks would interfere with flights from and into Los Angeles? How many years ago would that have seemed farcical and fantastical?

But now that's a real thing.

In your negotiation, you can think bigger. Think in terms of abundance; there is more than enough for everybody.

I don't want you to walk away from this thinking negotiation is a bunch of woo-woo stuff.

I don't want you to finish this book thinking that there isn't woo-woo in negotiation, because there is.

Knowing what you want—putting yourself in that mind frame, making sure that you feel strong in yourself and confident in asking for more of what you want will help you ensure that you get more of what you want.

Find within yourself the power to stand up for that and to expect more.

# ACKNOWLEDGMENTS

Writing this book though challenging at times has been a joyous experience. It wasn't necessarily the writing or the recording of it that made it an incredible experience. It was all the amazing people who helped make this book possible. And I want to thank them individually.

First, I thank God for everything in my life. I especially thank Him for bringing Roxanne Uken into my life. Through her, I was saved. I reconnected with my hopes and dreams. I cannot imagine what my life would have been like if she had not found me, challenged me to write down those four audacious goals, and pushed me to never forget them. We stayed connected for several years but, eventually, lost touch. Though she no longer is with us, I think of her daily and speak of her often. I am eternally grateful for her ongoing presence in my life. I want to thank her son, Bart, for continuing her legacy. Roxanne will forever be one of my guardian angels. Without her in my life, none of this would have happened.

I want to thank my amazing and wonderful husband, Keith. His unwavering love and support gives me strength. He believes in me always and has shown support in so many ways. I am honored to be his loving wife and cherish our partnership in life and business.

I want to give a special thank you to my daughters. First, since she was instrumental in making this book happen, I want to thank Lyra McKay. She took all the recordings that were used to create the book and did the initial rough edits. She also created the first cover concepts. Every day, she brings her brilliance and creativity to Venn Negotiation. Brianne shows care and love in all that she does and is a constant supporter and cheerleader. Danielle brings her brilliant marketing mind and calls me out when needed. You all push me to be better! Thank you for walking this journey with me all these years.

I also want to thank Merav Richter, Founder of Maverick Productions Inc., who took the rough edit that Lyra and I had developed, and really crafted it into a book. Her wisdom and guidance have been miraculous. We believe this book has the potential to be impact so many lives. A lot of that is because of Merav and her team's efforts.

I also want to thank Theresa Puskar. Theresa took my idea and turned it into something we could really work with. She developed the initial outline and interview questions, and we recorded the book first. We worked with amazing Gary Yek in Chicago to record this book. To make it an even better reading experience, we took the recording, and use that as the basis of this book. Without Theresa's guidance, and expertise coupled with Gary's genius as an audio engineer, we wouldn't have gotten this off the ground. Through this process, I learned that I record books a lot more easily than I write them. I am eternally grateful for the contributions that Theresa and Gary made to making this book a reality.

I also want to thank one of my key mentors, Blair Dunkley, for providing me a different language with which I can describe negotiation and communication. Blair's teachings have been instrumental in driving my own learning and influential in how I have built our VennMasters™ training programs.

Thank you to my team who has helped me in various capacities. Angel Tuccy for leading the way and helping me further my dream of writing a book. Thanks to your encouragement, I have others already in process. Melanie McSally for handling all my technology and implementing my website and deploying automation where appropriate. Farhana Cannon for assisting with social media and having her team heavily involved in cover designs. I also want to thank Lorenzo Alinsasaguin for creating the amazing cover art for my podcast, In the Venn Zone. We used his amazing work as a starting point for the book cover. The final cover was designed by Lucinda Kinch. Jennifer L. Horspool for pitching me and my stories to the press and media and for helping me step out in the biggest way. Imani Lee for helping make my videos look good. Jewels Duncan for helping me rethink my messaging and for showing me what being a goddess truly means.

From my youth, I want to thank Mr. (Lawrence) Greene, who taught me the power of independent thought. Mr. (Roy) Lackner challenged me to investigate myself and pushed me to be a go after what I wanted. I'd also like to thank Mr. (Bob) Quinn for being an incredible role model who taught me to be limited only by my dreams.

To some of my amazing professors who were there for me and my daughters during some very challenging times. Dr. Eric Gauger (Berkshire Community College) who saw me as a diamond in the rough and helped me find my shine. Mrs. Helen Plunkett (Berkshire Community College) who invited us for tea and luncheons and showed us a different way of living from the warmth of her own home. Dr. Barry Taylor (Rensselaer Polytechnic Institute), who bought groceries and led one of my favorite classes and was a huge advocate for me. At Harvard Business School, I'd like to thank my negotiations professors, James Sebenius and Kathleen Valley. I'd also like to thank Nancy Koehn. All three of these incredible people challenged me in ways that I didn't understand at the time. I am a better person and professional because of them.

Thank to Jillian Michaels and her entire team, especially Ash. I have enjoyed every moment of my conversations with Jillian, and Ash has been amazing. Jillian - thank you so much for lending your voice to this project.

Finally, I thank my parents for all that they taught me and my brother for his constant support through thick and thin.

My journey has been long, and I could not have done it without the support of so many people. I am certain to have omitted many people. Thankfully, another book is coming, and I will have another opportunity to say thank you! If I missed naming you here, know you are still precious to me and your imprint on my life has been meaningful.

# ABOUT THE AUTHOR

Christine McKay empowers you to ask for what you want and provides you with the skills and tools needed to negotiate for it.

Having negotiated deals for a multitude of Fortune 500 companies spanning 53 countries, Christine's academic career culminated with her earning an MBA from Harvard University.

Her early career was in international mergers and acquisitions. She led various deals, including multiple privatization deals in Eastern and Western Europe, and has negotiated key strategic alliances in Southeast Asia.

Christine has negotiated across many industries, including software, manufacturing, oil and gas, telecommunications, and more. She has extensive experience across many aspects of the business. Christine has negotiated from the viewpoints of procurement, strategic sourcing, and sales.

She is a sought-after speaker on negotiation related topics and the host of "In the Venn Zone," a podcast which helps entrepreneurs learn more negotiation styles and techniques.

In this groundbreaking book, and the accompanying program, she reveals powerful secrets on how to begin and end negotiation with your self-esteem and integrity intact, how to determine your personal negotiation style, and assess and adapt to the other side of the deal.

In this book, you will find quick tips on how to ask for what you really want, creative ways to reduce risk, a simple formula for demystifying contracts, how to genuinely ask for what you want instead of settling, and how to build and maintain solid relationships in and after the negotiation practice.

Christine's passion is finding common ground, levelling the playing field, and resolving complex issues on behalf of her clients.

# CHARITABLE PARTNER PROCEEDS

A percentage of the proceeds from the sale of this book go to - SHE IS HOPE LA.

SHE IS HOPE LA is an acronym that stands for Single Moms, Housing & Empowerment Inspiring Self-Confidence (through) Hope, Opportunity, Perseverance & Education (in) Los Angeles.

This 501(c)(3) nonprofit was founded to educate and empower single mothers starting over in the workplace and provide affordable, transitional housing and childcare.

SHE IS HOPE LA (SIHLA) does this using a three pronged approach:

1 Education via the SHE IS...Series which was designed to create opportunities for women to become what she believes SHE IS. This is done through a series of events including networking, panel discussions, in person meeting and building community for single moms and their kids. Topics included are

legal and financial advice, job training and preparation, mind-body wellness and peer support.

2 Jobs and job training through SHE IS HOPE Realty which is a full service brokerage serving all of California. If they are interested, single moms can learn to become a real estate agent or office support staff or they can choose to work at SHE IS HOPE LA Boutique learning customer service and retail sales skills. SIHLA also offers resume building and interview preparation and the Boutique will offer professional attire.

3 Housing - through grants, sponsors and donations, SIHLA will purchase a small apartment building to provide short term housing for their program participants while they rebuild their credit and self esteem.

A percentage of every transaction from SHE IS HOPE Realty goes back to SIHLA. Between that and the sales from the Boutique, SHE IS HOPE LA will eventually be self sustaining. Annual fundraisers will be held to boost awareness of the mission and help them expand into every major city in the United States.

Made in the USA
Middletown, DE
25 September 2021